· 国家社科基金项目"律师法实施问题研究"
· 国家"2011计划"司法文明协同创新中心研究成果
· 司法部2015年国家法治与法学理论研究项目"以律师为主体的公共法律服务体系构建模式研究"成果
· 2016年度中华全国律师协会重点研究课题"律师管理体制比较研究"成果

加拿大不列颠哥伦比亚省1998年法律职业法

王进喜 ◎ 译

中国法制出版社
CHINA LEGAL PUBLISHING HOUSE

译　序

　　律师传统上对自己的规制享有很大程度的控制。尽管在澳大利亚、英格兰和威尔士等地域，新自由主义国家在规制法律服务方面发挥着越来越突出的作用，律师的自我规制通常被"共同规制"所取代。但是在加拿大普通法地区，律师的自我规制生机勃勃。在加拿大的 10 个省和 3 个领地，都有一个律师协会。这些组织由律师领导，由律师选择，对其各自省份和领地的法律服务规制，行使极其完整的控制权。这些律师协会是由省立法确立的。这些法律赋予律师协会以充分的权力和裁量权，并且通常根据律师协会本身提出的建议进行修改。法官、立法者和政府官员，在加拿大法律服务规制中的作用相当小。因此，加拿大的律师管理体制是很独特的，即使是与其接壤的美国相比，也有着鲜明的特色。

　　当前我国司法改革如火如荼，围绕律师管理体制的改革也在进行中。例如，2016 年 6 月，中共中央办公厅、国务院办公厅印发了《关于深化律师制度改革的意见》；2016 年 12 月，司法部出台了《关于进一步加强律师协会建设的意见》；《律师法》的修改也正在进行中。因此，加强相关立法的比较研究，对于深化律师制度改革，促进律师事业发展无疑具有重要意义。

　　是为序。

王进喜

2017 年 4 月

Contents

Legal Profession Act ·· 002

   Definitions ·· 002

   Application ·· 010

Part 1   Organization ··· 012

  Division 1   Law Society ··· 012

   Incorporation ·· 012

   Object and duty of society ··· 012

   Benchers ·· 014

   Appointed benchers ·· 016

   Meetings ·· 016

   Elections ·· 018

   Officers and employees ·· 018

  Division 2   Committees ··· 020

   Law Society committees ··· 020

   Executive committee ··· 020

  Division 3   Rules and Resolutions ··· 022

   Law Society rules ··· 022

   Rules requiring membership approval ·· 024

   Implementing resolutions of general meeting ······························· 026

目录

法律职业法 ·· 003

  定义 ·· 003

  适用 ·· 011

第 1 节　组织 ·· 013

  第 1 目　律师协会 ·· 013

    成立 ·· 013

    律师协会的目标和职责 ···································· 013

    主管委员 ·· 015

    任命的主管委员 ·· 017

    会议 ·· 017

    选举 ·· 019

    职员和雇员 ·· 019

  第 2 目　委员会 ·· 021

    律师协会委员会 ·· 021

    执行委员会 ·· 021

  第 3 目　规则和决议 ·· 023

    律师协会规则 ·· 023

    需要得到会员批准的规则 ·································· 025

    全体会议的决议贯彻 ······································ 027

Part 2 Membership and Authority to Practise Law··············028

  Division 1 Practice of Law ··028

    Members··028

    Authority to practise law ···030

    Interprovincial practice··032

    Practitioners of foreign law ··036

    Association with non-resident lawyers or law firms·····················036

  Division 2 Admission and Reinstatement································038

    Applications for enrolment, call and admission, or reinstatement········038

    Articled students ··040

    Admission, reinstatement and requalification ······························040

    Prohibition on resignation from membership······························042

    Credentials hearings ··042

  Division 3 Fees and Assessments ···································044

    Annual fees and practising certificate ·······································044

    Fees and assessments ··048

    Failure to pay fee or penalty ···050

Part 3 Protection of the Public·····································052

    Complaints from the public ···052

    Suspension during investigation···054

    Medical examination ··058

    Written notification to chief judge ··058

    Practice standards ··060

    Education ··066

    Specialization and restricted practice···066

    Insurance··068

第2节　会员和从事法律执业活动的权力 …………………029

　第1目　法律执业活动 …………………029

　　会员 …………………029

　　从事法律执业活动的权力 …………………031

　　跨省执业 …………………033

　　外国法执业者 …………………037

　　与非本地律师或者律师事务所的联合 …………………037

　第2目　准入和恢复执业 …………………039

　　申请注册、认许和准入或者恢复执业 …………………039

　　见习生 …………………041

　　准入、恢复执业和恢复资格 …………………041

　　禁止退会 …………………043

　　资质听证 …………………043

　第3目　规费和摊款 …………………045

　　年度规费和执业证书 …………………045

　　规费和摊款 …………………049

　　未能支付规费或者罚金 …………………051

第3节　保护公众 …………………053

　　公众投诉 …………………053

　　在调查期间停止执业 …………………055

　　医学检查 …………………059

　　向首席法官发出书面通知 …………………059

　　执业标准 …………………061

　　教育 …………………067

　　专业化和限定执业领域 …………………067

　　保险 …………………069

Repealed ·· 074

Financial responsibility ·· 074

Trust accounts ·· 076

Unclaimed trust money ·· 078

Restriction on suspended and disbarred lawyers ················· 082

Part 4 Discipline ··· 084

Discipline rules ··· 084

Search and seizure ··· 086

Personal records in investigation or seizure ······················· 090

Discipline hearings ··· 090

Suspension ·· 098

Repealed ·· 100

Part 5 Hearings and Appeals ··· 102

Panels ·· 102

Failure to attend ·· 102

Right to counsel ·· 104

Witnesses ·· 104

Application of Administrative Tribunals Act ······················· 108

Repealed ·· 110

Society request for evidence ·· 110

Costs ·· 116

Review on the record ··· 118

Appeal ··· 120

废止 ·· 075

经济责任 ·· 075

信托账户 ·· 077

无人领取的信托资金 ······························ 079

对被停止执业和取消律师资格的律师的限制 ········ 083

第 4 节　惩戒 ···································· 085

惩戒规则 ·· 085

搜查和扣押 ·· 087

调查或者扣押的个人记录 ·························· 091

惩戒听证 ·· 091

停止执业 ·· 099

废止 ·· 101

第 5 节　听证和上诉 ······························ 103

专责小组 ·· 103

未能出席 ·· 103

获得律师帮助权 ···································· 105

证人 ·· 105

《行政裁判庭法》的适用 ·························· 109

废止 ·· 111

律师协会请求证据 ································ 111

成本 ·· 117

记录审查 ·· 119

上诉 ·· 121

Part 6   Custodianships ·································· 124

Definitions ··· 124

Appointment of custodian ···················· 126

If society appointed as custodian ··········· 132

Powers of custodian ··························· 132

Society access to property ···················· 134

Property in the custody of a custodian ····· 136

Applications to the court ····················· 138

Custodianship rules ··························· 140

Liability and costs ····························· 140

Part 7   Law Foundation ··························· 142

Definitions ·· 142

Law Foundation of British Columbia ········ 142

Board of governors ··························· 142

Bylaws ·· 146

Application of fund ··························· 148

Interest on trust accounts ···················· 150

Security and investment of trust funds ····· 154

Part 8   Lawyers' Fees ···························· 162

Definitions and interpretation ··············· 162

Agreement for legal services ················· 164

Contingent fee agreement ··················· 164

Restrictions on contingent fee agreements ··· 168

Examination of an agreement ··············· 170

Lawyer's bill ···································· 172

第 6 节 保管 ································ 125

定义 ································ 125

指定保管人 ································ 127

如果律师协会被指定为保管人 ················ 133

保管人的权力 ································ 133

律师协会近用财产 ································ 135

保管人保管的财产 ································ 137

向法院提出申请 ································ 139

保管规则 ································ 141

责任和成本 ································ 141

第 7 节 法律基金会 ························ 143

定义 ································ 143

不列颠哥伦比亚法律基金会 ················ 143

理事 ································ 143

章程 ································ 147

基金使用 ································ 149

信托账户的利息 ································ 151

信托基金的安全和投资 ························ 155

第 8 节 律师费 ································ 163

定义和解释 ································ 163

法律服务协议 ································ 165

风险代理费协议 ································ 165

对风险代理费协议的限制 ····················· 169

对协议的检查 ································ 171

律师的账单 ································ 173

Review of a lawyer's bill ·· 174

Matters to be considered by the registrar on a review ················ 178

Costs of a review of a lawyer's bill ································· 182

Remedies that may be ordered by the registrar ···················· 182

Refund of fee overpayment ·· 186

Appeal ·· 186

Registrar's certificate ·· 186

Order to deliver bill or property ····································· 188

Change of lawyer ··· 190

Lawyer's right to costs out of property recovered ················· 190

Part 9   Incorporation ··· 194

Definitions ·· 194

Authorized and prohibited activities of law corporations ··········· 194

Law corporation permit ·· 196

Law corporation rules ·· 200

Limited liability partnerships ·· 204

Responsibility of lawyers ··· 204

Part 10   General ·· 208

Enforcement ·· 208

Protection against actions ·· 210

Certain matters privileged ·· 210

Non-disclosure of privileged and confidential information ·········· 214

Repealed ·· 218

Service ·· 220

Law society insurance ··· 220

律师的账单的审查 ································· 175

司法常务官在审查时考虑的事项 ··············· 179

对律师的账单进行审查的成本 ················· 183

司法常务官可以命令的救济措施 ··············· 183

退还多付费用 ································· 187

上诉 ··· 187

司法常务官的证明 ····························· 187

命令提交账单或者财产 ························· 189

更换律师 ····································· 191

律师从追回的财产中取得成本的权利 ··········· 191

第 9 节　公司 ····································· 195

定义 ··· 195

法律公司的受权和被禁止活动 ················· 195

法律公司许可证 ······························· 197

法律公司规则 ································· 201

有限责任合伙 ································· 205

律师的责任 ··································· 205

第 10 节　一般规定 ································· 209

执行 ··· 209

针对诉讼的保护 ······························· 211

受特免权保护的某些事项 ····················· 211

不得披露受特免权保护的信息和秘密信息 ······· 215

废止 ··· 219

送达 ··· 221

律师协会保险 ································· 221

Legal archives···220

Part 11 Transitional and Consequential Provisions ············224

Repealed ···224

Spent···224

Commencement ··224

Legal Profession Act··226

Changes Not in Force ···226

Changes in Force··228

法律档案 ······································· 221

第 11 节　过渡性和相应规定 ····················· 225

废止 ··· 225

失效 ··· 225

施行 ··· 225

立法变动表 ······································ 227

尚未生效的变动 ··························· 227

生效的变动 ································· 229

重要译名对照表 ································· 230

This Act has "Not in Force" sections. See the Table of Legislative Changes.

Legal Profession Act

[SBC 1998] CHAPTER 9

Assented to May 13, 1998

Definitions

1 (1) In this Act:

"applicant" means a person who has applied for

(a) enrolment as an articled student,

(b) call and admission, or

(c) reinstatement;

"articled student" means a person enrolled in the society's admission program;

"bencher" means a person elected or appointed under Part 1 to serve as a member of the governing body of the society;

"chair" means a person appointed to preside at meetings of a committee or panel;

"conduct unbecoming a lawyer" includes a matter, conduct or thing that is considered, in the judgment of the benchers, a panel or a review board,

(a) to be contrary to the best interest of the public or of the legal profession, or

(b) to harm the standing of the legal profession;

"disbar" means to declare that a lawyer or former lawyer is unsuitable

本法含有"未生效"条文。参见立法变动表。

法律职业法

[不列颠哥伦比亚制定法 1998 年]第 9 章

1998 年 5 月 13 日获得御准

定义

1 （1）在本法中：

"申请人" 是指下列人员：

  （a）申请作为见习生注册的人员；

  （b）申请认许和准入的人员，或者

  （c）申请恢复执业的人员；

"见习生" 是指注册参加律师协会准入计划的人员；

"主管委员" 是指根据第 1 节被选举或者任命担任律师协会治理组织成员的人员；

"主席" 是指被任命来主持委员会或者专责小组会议的人员；

"与律师身份不相称的行为" 包括根据主管委员、专责小组或者审查委员会的判断，会导致下列情况的事项、行为或者物品：

  （a）有悖于公众或者法律职业的最大利益，或者

  （b）有损于法律职业的身份；

"取消律师资格" 是指宣布律师或者前律师不适合从事法律执业活

to practise law and to terminate the lawyer's membership in the society;

"**executive committee**" means the committee established under section 10;

"**executive director**" means the executive director or acting executive director of the society;

"**foundation**" means the Law Foundation of British Columbia continued under section 58 (1);

"**law corporation**" means a corporation that holds a valid permit under Part 9;

"**law firm**" means a legal entity or combination of legal entities carrying on the practice of law;

"**lawyer**" means a member of the society, and

>   (a) in Part 2, Division 1, includes a member of the governing body of the legal profession in another province or territory of Canada who is authorized to practise law in that province or territory,
>
>   (b) in Parts 4 to 6 and 10 includes a former member of the society, and
>
>   (c) in Part 10 includes an articled student;

"**member**" means a member of the society;

"**officer**" means the executive director, deputy executive director or other person appointed as an officer of the society by the benchers;

"**panel**" means a panel appointed in accordance with section 41;

"**practice of law**" includes

>   (a) appearing as counsel or advocate,
>
>   (b) drawing, revising or settling
>
>>   (i) a petition, memorandum, notice of articles or articles

动，并终止其在律师协会的成员资格；

"执行委员会" 是指根据第 10 条建立的委员会；

"执行主任" 是指律师协会的执行主任或者代理执行主任；

"基金会" 是指根据 58（1）存续的不列颠哥伦比亚法律基金会；

"法律公司" 是指根据第 9 节持有有效许可证的公司；

"律师事务所" 是指开展法律执业活动的法律实体或者法律实体的联合；

"律师" 是指律师协会的会员，并且：

（a）在第 2 节第 1 目，包括加拿大其他省或者领地的法律职业治理组织的被授权在该省或者领地从事法律执业活动的会员，

（b）在第 4 节至第 6 节和第 10 节，包括律师协会的前会员，以及

（c）在第 10 节，包括见习生；

"会员" 是指律师协会的会员；

"职员" 是指被主管委员任命为律师协会职员的执行主任、执行副主任或者其他人员；

"专责小组" 是指遵照第 41 条任命的专责小组；

"法律执业活动" 包括：

（a）作为法律顾问或者诉辩者出庭，

（b）起草、修改或者确定：

（i）《商业公司法》规定的申请、备忘录、章程细则或

under the Business Corporations Act, or an application, statement, affidavit, minute, resolution, bylaw or other document relating to the incorporation, registration, organization, reorganization, dissolution or winding up of a corporate body,

(ii) a document for use in a proceeding, judicial or extrajudicial,

(iii) a will, deed of settlement, trust deed, power of attorney or a document relating to a probate or a grant of administration or the estate of a deceased person,

(iv) a document relating in any way to a proceeding under a statute of Canada or British Columbia, or

(v) an instrument relating to real or personal estate that is intended, permitted or required to be registered, recorded or filed in a registry or other public office,

(c) doing an act or negotiating in any way for the settlement of, or settling, a claim or demand for damages,

(d) agreeing to place at the disposal of another person the services of a lawyer,

(e) giving legal advice,

(f) making an offer to do anything referred to in paragraphs (a) to (e), and

(g) making a representation by a person that he or she is qualified or entitled to do anything referred to in paragraphs (a) to (e),

but does not include

者章程，或者与法人团体的设立、登记、组织、重组、解散或者了结有关的申请、声明、宣誓陈述书、会议记录、决议、章程或者其他文件，

（ii）用于司法或者司法外程序的文件，

（iii）与遗嘱或者授权管理遗产或死者遗产有关的遗嘱、财产处分契据、信托契据、授权委托书或者文件，

（iv）以任何方式与根据加拿大或者不列颠哥伦比亚制定法规定的程序有关的文件，或者

（v）与动产或者不动产有关的用于经许可或者需要在登记处或者其他公署登记、记录或者存档的文书，

（c）为解决或者和解索赔或者损害赔偿要求，以任何方式采取行动或者谈判，

（d）同意由他人使用律师的服务，

（e）提供法律建议，

（f）提出从事（a）至（e）所称的任何活动，以及

（g）由有资格或者有权从事（a）至（e）的任何活动的人员就此点作出陈述，

但是并不包括：

(h) any of those acts if performed by a person who is not a lawyer and not for or in the expectation of a fee, gain or reward, direct or indirect, from the person for whom the acts are performed,

(i) the drawing, revising or settling of an instrument by a public officer in the course of the officer's duty,

(j) the lawful practice of a notary public,

(k) the usual business carried on by an insurance adjuster who is licensed under Division 2 of Part 6 of the Financial Institutions Act, or

(l) agreeing to do something referred to in paragraph (d), if the agreement is made under a prepaid legal services plan or other liability insurance program;

"practising lawyer" means a member in good standing who holds or is entitled to hold a practising certificate;

"president" means the chief elected official of the society;

"resolution" means a motion passed by a majority of those voting at a meeting;

"respondent" means a person whose conduct or competence is the subject of a hearing or an appeal under this Act;

"review board" means a review board appointed in accordance with section 47;

"rules" means rules enacted by the benchers under this Act;

"society" means the Law Society of British Columbia continued under section 2;

"suspension" means temporary disqualification from the practice of law;

（h）不是律师的人员从事的且不是直接或者间接为了或者期待从接受所从事的行为的人员那里取得律师费、收益或者回报的行为，

（i）公务员在履行其职责期间起草、修改或者校定文书，

（j）公证人的合法执业活动，

（k）根据《金融机构法》第 6 节第 2 目持照的保险精算人开展的通常业务，或者

（l）根据预付法律服务计划或者其他责任保险计划中的协议，从事（d）所称的某些活动；

"执业律师"是指持有或者有权持有执业证书的资格完好的会员；

"会长"是指律师协会的首席选任官员；

"决议"是指在会议中多数人投票通过的动议；

"应诉人"是指其行为或者称职性是根据本法进行的听证或者上诉的主题的人员；

"审查委员会"是指遵照第 47 条任命的审查委员会；

"规则"是指主管委员根据本法制定的规则；

"律师协会"是指根据第 2 条存续的不列颠哥伦比亚律师协会；

"停止执业"是指临时取消从事法律执业活动的资格；

"written" or "in writing" includes written messages communicated electronically.

(2) In Parts 1 to 5, **"costs"** means costs assessed under a rule made under section 27 (2)(e) or 46.

Application

1.1　This Act does not apply to a person who is both a lawyer and a part time judicial justice, as that term is defined in section 1 of the Provincial Court Act, in the person's capacity as a part time judicial justice under that Act.

"书面的"或者**"以书面形式"**包括以电子方式交流的书面讯息。

（2）在第 1 节至第 5 节，**"成本"**是指根据 27（2）（e）或者第 46 条制定的规则加以评定的成本。

适用

1.1　本法并不适用于既是律师又是兼职法官（该术语的定义见《省法院法》第 1 条）并根据该法以兼职法官身份出现的人员。

Part 1 **Organization**

Division 1 Law Society

Incorporation

2 (1) The Law Society of British Columbia is continued.

  (2) For the purposes of this Act, the society has all the powers and capacity of a natural person.

Object and duty of society

3 It is the object and duty of the society to uphold and protect the public interest in the administration of justice by

  (a) preserving and protecting the rights and freedoms of all persons,

  (b) ensuring the independence, integrity, honour and competence of lawyers,

  (c) establishing standards and programs for the education, professional responsibility and competence of lawyers and of applicants for call and admission,

  (d) regulating the practice of law, and

第 1 节 组织

第 1 目 律师协会

成立

2 （1）不列颠哥伦比亚律师协会继续存在。

（2）就本法目的而言，律师协会有自然人的全部权能。

律师协会的目标和职责

3 律师协会的目标和职责是，通过下列活动，维持和保护司法中
的公共利益：

（a）维护所有人的权利和自由，

（b）确保律师的独立性、适正性、尊严和称职性，

（c）就律师与认许和准入的申请人的教育、职业责任和称职性
建立标准和计划，

（d）规制法律执业活动，以及

(e) supporting and assisting lawyers, articled students and lawyers of other jurisdictions who are permitted to practise law in British Columbia in fulfilling their duties in the practice of law.

Benchers

4　(1) The following are benchers:

(a) the Attorney General;

(b) the persons appointed under section 5;

(c) the lawyers elected under section 7;

(d) the president, first vice-president and second vice-president.

(2) The benchers govern and administer the affairs of the society and may take any action they consider necessary for the promotion, protection, interest or welfare of the society.

(3) The benchers may take any action consistent with this Act by resolution.

(4) Subsections (2) and (3) are not limited by any specific power or responsibility given to the benchers by this Act.

(5) The benchers may

(a) use the fees, assessments and other funds of the society, including funds previously collected or designated for a special purpose before this Act came into force, for the purposes of the society,

(b) raise funds by the issue of debentures, with or without a trust deed, for the purposes of the society,

(c) provide for a pension scheme for its officers and

（e）支持和帮助律师、见习生和为履行其在法律执业活动中的职责而被允许在不列颠哥伦比亚从事法律执业活动的其他司法辖区的律师。

主管委员

4　（1）下列人员是主管委员：

（a）检察长；

（b）根据第 5 条任命的人员；

（c）根据第 7 条选举的律师；

（d）会长、第一副会长和第二副会长。

（2）主管委员治理和管理律师协会的事务，并可以采取他们认为促进、保护律师协会的利益或者福祉所必需的任何行动。

（3）主管委员可以通过决议采取任何与本法一致的行动。

（4）（2）和（3）并不受到本法赋予主管委员的任何具体权力或者责任的限制。

（5）主管委员可以：

（a）为律师协会之目的，使用律师协会的规费、摊款和其他资金，包括在本法生效前为特定目的收集的或者指定的资金，

（b）为律师协会之目的，通过发行金融债券（无论有无信托契约）筹集资金，

（c）用律师协会的资金为其职员和雇员提供退休金计划，以及

employees out of the funds of the society, and

(d) approve forms to be used for the purposes of this Act.

Appointed benchers

5 (1) The Lieutenant Governor in Council may appoint up to 6 persons to be benchers.

(2) Members and former members of the society are not eligible to be appointed under this section.

(3) A bencher appointed under this section has all the rights and duties of an elected bencher, unless otherwise stated in this Act.

(4) If a bencher appointed under this section fails to complete a term of office, the Lieutenant Governor in Council may appoint a replacement to hold office for the balance of the term of the bencher who left office.

(5) A bencher appointed under this section is not eligible to hold the position of president, first vice-president or second vice-president.

Meetings

6 (1) The benchers may make rules respecting meetings of the benchers.

(2) For a quorum at a meeting of the benchers, at least 7 benchers must be present and a majority of those present must be members of the society.

(3) A motion assented to in writing by at least 75% of the benchers

（d）批准为本法之目的所使用的表单。

任命的主管委员

5　（1）省督可以任命最多 6 人担任主管委员。

（2）律师协会的会员和前会员无资格根据本条获得任命。

（3）根据本条任命的主管委员拥有选任主管的全部权利和职责，除非本法另有规定。

（4）如果根据本条任命的主管委员未能完成一个任期，省督可以任命替代者就任离职的主管委员的剩余任期。

（5）根据本条任命的主管委员无资格担任会长、第一副会长或者第二副会长。

会议

6　（1）主管委员可以就主管委员会议制定规则。

（2）就主管委员会议的法定人数而言，至少 7 名主管委员必须出席，且其多数必须是律师协会会员。

（3）至少 75% 的主管委员以书面形式同意的动议，与主管委员

has the same effect as a resolution passed at a regularly convened meeting of the benchers.

Elections

7 (1) The benchers may make rules respecting the election of benchers and of the second vice-president.

(2) The rules made under subsection (1) must be consistent with the following:

(a) voting is by secret ballot;

(b) the right of each member to vote for a bencher or the second vice-president carries the same weight as any other member who is entitled to vote for that bencher or the second vice-president;

(c) only members in good standing are entitled to vote.

(3) Section 11 (4) applies to the rules made under subsection (1) of this section unless they deal directly with a matter referred to in section 12.

(4) Section 12 applies to the rules made under subsection (1) of this section that deal directly with a matter referred to in that section.

Officers and employees

8 The benchers may make rules to do either or both of the following:

(a) delegate to the executive director, or the executive director's delegate, any power or authority of the

定期召开的会议通过的决议具有同等效力。

选举

7 （1）主管委员可以就主管委员和第二副会长的选举制定规则。

（2）根据（1）制定的规则必须与下列事项保持一致：

（a）通过无记名投票进行选举；

（b）每个会员就主管委员或者第二副会长进行投票的权利
与任何其他有权就主管委员或者第二副会长进行投票
的会员的权利相同；

（c）只有资格完好的会员有权投票。

（3）11（4）适用于根据本条（1）制定的规则，除非它们直接
处理的是第 12 条所称事项。

（4）第 12 条适用于根据本条（1）制定的直接处理该条所称事
项的规则。

职员和雇员

8 主管委员可以制定规则，从事下列活动之一或者二者：

（a）将主管委员根据本法拥有的任何权力或者权限委派
给执行主任或者执行主任的委派代表，规则制定权

benchers under this Act except rule-making authority;

(b) authorize a committee established under this Act to delegate authority granted to it under this Act to the executive director or the executive director's delegate.

Division 2 Committees

Law Society committees

9 (1) The benchers may establish committees in addition to those established by this Act.

(2) The benchers may authorize a committee to do any act or to exercise any jurisdiction that, by this Act, the benchers are authorized to do or to exercise, except the exercise of rule-making authority.

(3) The benchers may make rules providing for

(a) the appointment and termination of appointments of persons to committees, and

(b) the practice and procedure for meetings of committees, including proceedings before committees.

(4) For a quorum at a meeting of a committee, at least 1/2 of the members of the committee must be present.

Executive committee

10 (1) The benchers must establish an executive committee.

除外；

（b）授权根据本法成立的委员会将根据本法赋予它的权限委派给执行主任或者执行主任的委派代表。

第 2 目 　委员会

律师协会委员会

9 （1）除了本法建立的委员会之外，主管委员可以建立委员会。

（2）主管委员可以授权委员会从事或者行使本法授权主管委员从事的任何行为或者行使的任何管辖权，行使制定规则的权力除外。

（3）主管委员可以制定规则，规定下列事项：

（a）委员会成员的任命和终止任命，以及

（b）委员会会议的操作和程序，包括委员会之前的程序。

（4）就委员会会议的法定人数而言，至少委员会成员的 1/2 必须出席。

执行委员会

10 （1）主管委员必须建立执行委员会。

(2) The benchers may delegate any of the powers and duties of the benchers to the executive committee, subject to any conditions they consider necessary.

(3) A quorum of the executive committee is 4.

(4) A motion assented to in writing by at least 75% of the executive committee's members has the same effect as a resolution passed at a regularly convened meeting of the executive committee.

Division 3   Rules and Resolutions

Law Society rules

11 (1) The benchers may make rules for the governing of the society, lawyers, law firms, articled students and applicants, and for the carrying out of this Act.

(2) Subsection (1) is not limited by any specific power or requirement to make rules given to the benchers by this Act.

(3) The rules are binding on the society, lawyers, law firms, the benchers, articled students, applicants and persons referred to in section 16 (2) (a) or 17 (1) (a) .

(4) Enactment, amendment or rescission of a rule is not effective unless at least 2/3 of the benchers present at the meeting at which the rule, amendment or rescission is considered vote in favour of it.

(5) Unless section 12 applies, no approval other than that required under subsection (4) of this section is necessary to

（2）主管委员可以在其认为必要的任何条件之下，将主管委员的任何权力和职责委派给执行委员会。

（3）执行委员会的法定人数是 4 人。

（4）至少 75% 的执行委员会成员以书面形式同意的动议，与执行委员会定期召开的会议通过的决议具有同等效力。

第 3 目　规则和决议

律师协会规则

11（1）主管委员可以就律师协会、律师、律师事务所、主管委员、见习生、申请人的治理，以及本法的执行制定规则。

（2）（1）并不受到本法赋予主管委员制定规则的任何具体权力或者要求的限制。

（3）规则对律师协会、律师、律师事务所、主管委员、见习生、申请人和 16（2）（a）和 17（1）（a）所称人员有约束力。

（4）制定、修改或者废除规则无效，除非出席审议规则、修正或者废除会议的主管委员中至少 2/3 投票支持它。

（5）除非第 12 条适用，除了本条（4）之要求外，不需要就制定、废除或者修正规则获得批准。

enact, rescind or amend a rule.

Rules requiring membership approval

12 (1) The benchers must make rules respecting the following:

(a) the offices of president, first vice-president or second vice-president;

(b) the term of office of benchers;

(c) the removal of the president, first vice-president, second vice-president or a bencher;

(d) the electoral districts for the election of benchers;

(e) the eligibility to be elected and to serve as a bencher;

(f) the filling of vacancies among elected benchers;

(g) the general meetings of the society, including the annual general meeting;

(h) the appointment, duties and powers of the auditor of the society;

(i) life benchers;

(j) [Repealed 2012-16-6 (a) .]

(k) the qualifications to act as auditor of the society when an audit is required under this Act.

(2) The first rules made under subsection (1) after this Act comes into force must be consistent with the provisions of the Legal Profession Act, R.S.B.C. 1996, c. 255, relating to the same subject matter.

(3) The benchers may amend or rescind rules made under subsection (1) or enact new rules respecting the matters

需要得到会员批准的规则

12 （1）主管委员必须就下列事项制定规则：

（a）会长、第一副会长或者第二副会长职务；

（b）主管委员的职务任期；

（c）会长、第一副会长或者第二副会长或者主管委员的免职；

（d）选举主管委员的选区；

（e）被选举并担任主管委员的资格；

（f）选任主管委员缺位的填补；

（g）律师协会的全体会议，包括年度全体会议；

（h）律师协会的审计人员的任命、职责和权力；

（i）终身主管委员；

（j）[废止 2012-16-6（a）.]

（k）在根据本法需要进行审计时，担任律师协会审计人员的资格。

（2）在本法生效后根据（1）制定的第一套规则，必须与《法律职业法》（R.S.B.C. 1996，c. 255）在相同主题上的规定一致。

（3）遵照全体大会或者关于规则草案、规则的修正或者废除的公投中投票的 2/3 会员的赞成票，主管委员可修改或者

referred to in subsection (1) , in accordance with an affirmative vote of 2/3 of those members voting at a general meeting or in a referendum respecting the proposed rule, or the amendment or rescission of a rule.

Implementing resolutions of general meeting

13 (1) A resolution of a general meeting of the society is not binding on the benchers except as provided in this section.

(2) A referendum of all members must be conducted on a resolution if

(a) it has not been substantially implemented by the benchers within 12 months following the general meeting at which it was adopted, and

(b) the executive director receives a petition signed by at least 5% of members in good standing of the society requesting a referendum on the resolution.

(3) Subject to subsection (4) , the resolution is binding on the benchers if at least

(a) 1/3 of all members in good standing of the society vote in the referendum, and

(b) 2/3 of those voting vote in favour of the resolution.

(4) The benchers must not implement a resolution if to do so would constitute a breach of their statutory duties.

废除根据（1）制定的规则，或者就（1）所称事项制定新的规则。

全体会议的决议贯彻

13　（1）律师协会全体会议的决议对主管委员没有约束力，本条另有规定者除外。

（2）在下列情况下，就决议进行全体会员的公投：

（a）在采纳该决议的全体大会后 12 个月内，该决议没有得到主管委员的实质贯彻，并且

（b）执行主任收到了律师协会至少 5% 资格完好的会员签名的请愿书，请求就决议进行公投。

（3）在遵守（4）的情况下，在下列情况下，决议对主管委员有约束力：

（a）律师协会至少 1/3 资格完好的会员在公投中投票，并且

（b）这些表决票中至少 2/3 支持决议。

（4）主管委员不得贯彻将会违反其制定法职责的决议。

Part 2 Membership and Authority to Practise Law

Division 1 Practice of Law

Members

14 (1) The benchers may make rules to do any of the following:

(a) establish categories of members;

(b) determine the rights and privileges associated with categories of members;

(c) set the annual fee for categories of members other than practising lawyers;

(d) determine whether or not a person is a member in good standing of the society.

(2) A member in good standing of the society is an officer of all courts of British Columbia.

(3) A practising lawyer is entitled to use the style and title of "Notary Public in and for the Province of British Columbia", and has and may exercise all the powers, rights, duties and privileges of the office of notary public.

第 2 节　会员和从事法律执业活动的权力

第 1 目　法律执业活动

会员

14 （1）主管委员可以就任何下列事项制定规则：

　　（a）建立会员类别；

　　（b）确定与会员类别相关的权利和特权；

　　（c）确定执业律师之外的会员类别的年费；

　　（d）确定某人是否是律师协会资格完好的会员。

（2）律师协会资格完好的会员是不列颠哥伦比亚所有法院的
　　 职员。

（3）执业律师有权使用"不列颠哥伦比亚省公证人"之称谓
　　 和头衔，并拥有和可以行使公证人职务的全部权力、权
　　 利、职责和特权。

Authority to practise law

15 (1) No person, other than a practising lawyer, is permitted to engage in the practice of law, except

(a) a person who is an individual party to a proceeding acting without counsel solely on his or her own behalf,

(b) as permitted by the Court Agent Act,

(c) an articled student, to the extent permitted by the benchers,

(d) an individual or articled student referred to in section 12 of the Legal Services Society Act, to the extent permitted under that Act,

(e) a lawyer of another jurisdiction permitted to practise law in British Columbia under section 16 (2) (a) , to the extent permitted under that section,

(f) a practitioner of foreign law holding a permit under section 17 (1) (a) , to the extent permitted under that section, and

(g) a lawyer who is not a practising lawyer, to the extent permitted under the rules.

(2) A person who is employed by a practising lawyer, a law firm, a law corporation or the government and who acts under the supervision of a practising lawyer does not contravene subsection (1) .

(3) A person must not do any act described in paragraphs (a) to (g) of the definition of "practice of law" in section 1 (1) , even though the act is not performed for or in the

从事法律执业活动的权力

15 （1）除执业律师外，不得允许任何人从事法律执业活动，
      除非：
      （a）没有法律顾问而自行代理的程序的自然人当事人，

      （b）为《法院代理人法》所允许，
      （c）主管委员许可范围内的见习生，

      （d）《法律服务协会法》第 12 条所称的该法许可范围内
           的个人或者见习生，

      （e）根据 16（2）（a）允许，在该条许可的范围内，在不
           列颠哥伦比亚从事法律执业活动的其他司法辖区的
           律师，
      （f）根据 17（1）（a）持有许可证，在该条许可的范围内
           的外国法执业者，以及

      （g）规则许可范围内的不是执业律师的律师。

   （2）其行为在执业律师监督下的受雇于执业律师、律师事务
       所、法律公司或者政府的人员，并不违反（1）。

   （3）在下列情况下，任何人不得从事 1（1）中 "法律执业活
       动" 的定义中（a）至（g）规定的任何行为，即使从事
       该行为不是直接或者间接为了或者期待从接受所从事的

expectation of a fee, gain or reward, direct or indirect, from the person for whom the acts are performed, if

(a) the person is a member or former member of the society who is suspended or has been disbarred, or who, as a result of disciplinary proceedings, has resigned from membership in the society or otherwise ceased to be a member as a result of disciplinary proceedings, or

(b) the person is suspended or prohibited for disciplinary reasons from practising law in another jurisdiction.

(4) A person must not falsely represent himself, herself or any other person as being

(a) a lawyer,

(b) an articled student, a student-at-law or a law clerk, or

(c) a person referred to in subsection (1) (e) or (f) .

(5) Except as permitted in subsection (1) , a person must not commence, prosecute or defend a proceeding in any court.

(6) The benchers may make rules prohibiting lawyers from facilitating or participating in the practice of law by persons who are not authorized to practise law.

Interprovincial practice

16 (1) In this section, **"governing body"** means the governing body of the legal profession in another province or a territory of Canada.

(2) The benchers may permit qualified lawyers of other Canadian jurisdictions to practise law in British Columbia

行为的人员那里取得律师费、收益或者回报：

（a）该人作为律师协会会员或者前会员，被停止执业或者取消律师资格，或者作为惩戒程序的结果，已经从律师协会退会，或者作为惩戒程序的结果以其他方式不再是律师协会会员，或者

（b）该人因惩戒原因在其他司法辖区被停止执业或者禁止从事法律执业活动。

（4）任何人不得虚假宣示自己或者任何其他人是：

（a）律师，

（b）见习生、法学院学生或者法律助手，或者

（c）（1）（e）或者（f）所称的人员。

（5）除非为（1）所允许，任何人不得在任何法院启动程序或者就程序起诉或者辩护。

（6）主管委员可以制定规则，来禁止律师帮助或者参与无权从事法律执业活动的人员从事法律执业活动。

跨省执业

16　（1）在本条中，**"治理组织"** 是指加拿大其他省或者领地的法律职业的治理组织。

（2）主管委员可以允许加拿大其他司法辖区的合格律师在不列颠哥伦比亚从事法律执业活动，可以通过下列一个或

and may promote cooperation with the governing bodies of the legal profession in other Canadian jurisdictions by doing one or more of the following:

(a) permitting a lawyer or class of lawyers of another province or a territory of Canada to practise law in British Columbia;

(b) attaching conditions or limitations to a permission granted under paragraph (a);

(c) submitting disputes concerning the interjurisdictional practice of law to an independent adjudicator under an arbitration program established by agreement with one or more governing bodies;

(d) participating with one or more governing bodies in establishing and operating a fund to compensate members of the public for misappropriation or wrongful conversion by lawyers practising outside their home jurisdictions;

(e) making rules

(i) establishing conditions under which permission may be granted under paragraph (a), including payment of a fee,

(ii) respecting the enforcement of a fine imposed by a governing body, and

(iii) allowing release of information about a lawyer to a governing body, including information about practice restrictions, complaints, competency and discipline.

者多个活动，促进与加拿大其他司法辖区的法律职业治
理组织的合作：

（a）允许加拿大其他省或者领地的律师或者律师类别在
　　不列颠哥伦比亚从事法律执业活动；

（b）就根据（a）授予的许可设定条件或者限制；

（c）根据与一个或者多个治理组织达成的协议建立的仲
　　裁计划，将关于跨司法辖区法律执业活动的争端提
　　交独立裁判者；

（d）与一个或者多个治理组织一起建立和运营基金，以
　　就在其源地司法辖区之外执业的律师的挪用或者非
　　法侵占行为向公众进行赔偿；

（e）就下列事项制定规则：
　　（i）确立根据（a）可以作出的许可的条件，包括交
　　　　纳规费，

　　（ii）治理组织处以的罚款的执行，以及

　　（iii）允许向治理组织提供关于律师的信息，包括信
　　　　息执业限制、投诉、称职性和惩戒的信息。

(3) Parts 3 to 8 and 10 apply to a lawyer or class of lawyers given permission under this section.

Practitioners of foreign law

17　(1) The benchers may do any or all of the following:

(a) permit a person holding professional legal qualifications obtained in a country other than Canada to practise law in British Columbia;

(b) attach conditions or limitations to a permission granted under paragraph (a) ;

(c) make rules establishing conditions or limitations under which permission may be granted under paragraph (a) , including payment of a fee.

(2) Parts 3 to 8 and 10 apply to a person given permission under this section.

Association with non–resident lawyers or law firms

18　The benchers may make rules concerning the association of members of the society or law firms in British Columbia with lawyers or law firms in other jurisdictions.

（3）第 3 节至第 8 节和第 10 节，适用于根据本条获得许可的
　　律师或者律师类别。

外国法执业者

17　（1）主管委员可以从事下列任何或者全部活动：
　　　（a）允许持有在加拿大之外的其他国家获得的法律职业
　　　　　资格的人员在不列颠哥伦比亚从事法律执业活动；

　　　（b）对根据（a）授予的许可设定条件或者限制；

　　　（c）制定规则，就可以根据（a）作出的许可建立条件或
　　　　　者限制，包括交纳规费。

　　（2）第 3 节至第 8 节和第 10 节适用于根据本条获得许可的人员。

与非本地律师或者律师事务所的联合

18　主管委员可以就不列颠哥伦比亚律师协会会员或者律师事务
　　所与其他司法辖区的律师或者律师事务所的联合制定规则。

Division 2   Admission and Reinstatement

Applications for enrolment, call and admission, or reinstatement

19 (1) No person may be enrolled as an articled student, called and admitted or reinstated as a member unless the benchers are satisfied that the person is of good character and repute and is fit to become a barrister and a solicitor of the Supreme Court.

(2) On receiving an application for enrolment, call and admission or reinstatement, the benchers may

(a) grant the application,

(b) grant the application subject to any conditions or limitations to which the applicant consents in writing, or

(c) order a hearing.

(3) If an applicant for reinstatement is a person referred to in section 15 (3) (a) or (b) , the benchers must order a hearing.

(4) A hearing may be ordered, commenced or completed despite the applicant's withdrawal of the application.

(5) The benchers may vary conditions or limitations made under subsection (2) (b) if the applicant consents in writing to the variation.

第 2 目　准入和恢复执业

申请注册、认许和准入或者恢复执业

19　（1）任何人不得注册为见习生、认许和准入或者恢复执业为
　　　　会员，除非主管委员确信该人品性和声望良好，适合成
　　　　为最高法院的出庭律师和事务律师。

　　　（2）在收到注册、认许和准入或者恢复执业申请时，主管委
　　　　员可以：
　　　　（a）批准申请，
　　　　（b）批准申请，但是设定申请人以书面形式同意的任何
　　　　　　　条件或者限制，或者
　　　　（c）命令举行听证。
　　　（3）如果恢复执业申请人是 15（3）（a）或者（b）所称人员，
　　　　主管委员必须命令举行听证。

　　　（4）尽管申请被撤回，仍然可以命令进行听证、开始或者完
　　　　成听证。
　　　（5）如果申请人以书面形式同意变更，主管委员可以变更根
　　　　据（2）（b）设定的条件和限制。

Articled students

20 (1) The benchers may make rules to do any of the following:

(a) establish requirements, including academic requirements, and procedures for enrolment of articled students;

(b) set fees for enrolment;

(c) establish requirements for lawyers to serve as principals to articled students;

(d) limit the number of articled students who may be articled to a principal;

(e) stipulate the duties of principals and articled students;

(f) permit the investigation and consideration of the fitness of a lawyer to act as a principal to an articled student.

(2) The benchers may establish and maintain an educational program for articled students.

Admission, reinstatement and requalification

21 (1) The benchers may make rules to do any of the following:

(a) establish a credentials committee and delegate any or all authority and responsibility under this Part, other than rule-making authority, to that committee;

(b) establish requirements, including academic requirements, and procedures for call to the Bar of British Columbia and admission as a solicitor of the Supreme Court;

(c) set a fee for call and admission;

(d) establish requirements and procedures for the reinstatement

见习生

20　（1）主管委员可以就任何下列事项制定规则：

　　　（a）确立要求，包括见习生的学历要求和注册的程序；

　　　（b）确定注册规费；

　　　（c）就律师担任见习生的负责人确立要求；

　　　（d）限制负责人训练的见习生的数量；

　　　（e）规定负责人和见习生的职责；

　　　（f）允许调查和审议律师担任见习生的负责人的适当性。

　　（2）主管委员可以就见习生建立和维护教育计划。

准入、恢复执业和恢复资格

21　（1）主管委员可以就任何下列事项制定规则：

　　　（a）建立资质委员会，并将本节规定的任何或者全部权力和责任委派给该委员会，规则制定权除外；

　　　（b）就不列颠哥伦比亚出庭律师协会的认许和作为最高法院事务律师的准入建立要求（包括学历要求）和程序；

　　　（c）确定认许和准入规费；

　　　（d）就律师协会前会员恢复执业建立要求和程序；

of former members of the society;

（e）set a fee for reinstatement;

（f）establish conditions under which a member in good standing of the society who is not permitted to practise law, may apply to become a practising lawyer.

（2）The fee set under subsection（1）（c）must not exceed 1/6 of the practice fee set under section 23（1）（a）.

（3）The benchers may impose conditions or limitations on the practice of a lawyer who, for a cumulative period of 3 years of the 5 years preceding the imposition of the conditions, has not engaged in the practice of law.

Prohibition on resignation from membership

21.1　（1）A lawyer may not resign from membership in the society without the consent of the benchers if the lawyer is the subject of

（a）a citation or other discipline process under Part 4,

（b）an investigation under this Act, or

（c）a practice review under the rules.

（2）In granting consent under subsection（1）, the benchers may impose conditions.

Credentials hearings

22　（1）This section applies to a hearing ordered under section 19 （2）（c）.

（2）A hearing must be conducted before a panel.

（e）确定恢复执业规费；

（f）建立没有被许可从事法律执业活动的资格完好的律师
　　协会会员可以申请成为执业律师的条件。

（2）根据（1）（c）确定的规费，不得超过根据 23（1）（a）确
　　定的执业费的 1/6。

（3）主管委员可以就在设定条件前 5 年中累计 3 年没有从事
　　法律执业活动的律师的业务活动设定条件或者限制。

禁止退会

21.1　（1）在下列情况下，未经主管委员同意，律师不得从律师协
　　会退会：

（a）律师是第 4 节规定的传唤证或者其他惩戒程序的对象，

（b）律师受到根据本法进行的调查，或者

（c）律师受到根据规则进行的执业审查。

（2）在根据（1）作出同意时，主管委员可以设定条件。

资质听证

22　（1）本条适用于根据 19（2）（c）命令进行的听证。

（2）听证必须由专责小组进行。

(3) Following a hearing, the panel must do one of the following:

(a) grant the application;

(b) grant the application subject to conditions or limitations that the panel considers appropriate;

(c) reject the application.

(4) If an application is rejected,

(a) the panel must, on the written request of the applicant, give written reasons for its decision, and

(b) the applicant must not be enrolled as an articled student, called and admitted or reinstated as a member.

(5) On application, the benchers may vary or remove conditions or limitations imposed by a panel under this section.

(6) The benchers may make rules requiring payment of security for costs of a hearing.

Division 3   Fees and Assessments

Annual fees and practising certificate

23 (1) A practising lawyer must pay to the society an annual fee consisting of

(a) a practice fee in an amount set by the benchers, and

(b) [Repealed 2012-16-13.]

(c) an insurance fee set under section 30 (3) (a) , unless exempted from payment of the insurance fee under section 30 (4) (b) .

（3）在听证之后，专责小组必须采取下列措施之一：

　　（a）批准申请；

　　（b）批准申请，但是设定专责小组认为适当的条件或者限制；

　　（c）驳回申请。

（4）如果申请被驳回：

　　（a）经申请人书面请求，专责小组必须就其决定给出书面理由，并且

　　（b）申请人不得被注册为见习生、认许和准入或者恢复执业为会员。

（5）经申请，主管委员可以变更或者撤销专责小组根据本条设定的条件或者限制。

（6）主管委员可以制定规则，要求就听证的成本支付保证金。

第 3 目　规费和摊款

年度规费和执业证书

23　（1）执业律师必须向律师协会交纳由下列费用组成的年度规费：

　　（a）主管委员确定的执业规费，以及

　　（b）［废止 2012-16-13.］

　　（c）根据 30（3）（a）确定的保险费，除非根据 30（4）（b）免于支付保险费。

(2) The benchers may waive payment of all or part of the annual fee or a special assessment for a lawyer whom they wish to honour.

(3) A lawyer who is suspended under section 38 (5) (d) or the rules made under section 25 (2) , 32 (2) (b) , 36 (h) or 39 (1) (a) must pay the annual fee or special assessment when it is due in order to remain a member of the society.

(4) The executive director must issue to each practising lawyer a practising certificate on payment of the annual fee, if the lawyer is otherwise in good standing and has complied with this Act and the rules.

(5) A certificate purporting to contain the signature of the executive director stating that a person is, or was at the time specified in the certificate, a member in good standing of the society is proof of that fact, in the absence of evidence to the contrary.

(6) A lawyer who is suspended or who, for any other reason, ceases to be a member in good standing of the society must immediately surrender to the executive director his or her practising certificate and any proof of professional liability insurance issued by the society.

(7) The benchers may make rules to do any of the following:

(a) set the date by which the annual fee is payable, subject to rules made under section 30 (4) (a) ;

(b) permit late payment of the annual fee or a special assessment;

（2）为表示对某律师的敬重，主管委员可以放弃其缴纳的全部或者部分年度规费或者特别摊款。

（3）根据 38（5）（d）或者根据依 25（2）、32（2）（b）、36（h）或者 39（1）（a）制定的规则被停止执业的律师，为了保持其在律师协会的会员身份，必须交纳所欠年度规费或者特别摊款。

（4）在支付年度规费后，如果律师在其他方面资格完好，并且遵守了本法和规则，执行主任必须向执业律师颁发执业证书。

（5）在没有相反证据的情况下，载有执行主任签字，说明某人在证明具体说明的时间是或者曾经是律师协会资格完好的会员的证明，是关于该事实的证据。

（6）被停止执业的律师，或者因任何其他原因不再是律师协会资格完好的会员的律师，必须立即向执行主任交回其执业证书和律师协会签发的任何职业责任保险证明。

（7）主管委员可以就任何下列事项制定规则：

（a）在遵守根据 30（4）（a）制定的规则的情况下，确定交纳年度规费的日期；

（b）允许推迟交纳年度规费或者特别摊款；

(c) set a fee for late payment of fees and assessments;

(d) determine the circumstances in which a full or partial refund of a fee or assessment may be made;

(e) deem a lawyer to have been a practising lawyer during a period in which the lawyer was in default of payment of fees or an assessment on conditions that the benchers consider appropriate.

Fees and assessments

24 (1) The benchers may

(a) set fees, and

(b) set special assessments to be paid by lawyers and applicants for the purposes of the society and set the date by which they must be paid.

(c) [Repealed 2012-16-14.]

(2) [Repealed 2012-16-14.]

(3) If the benchers set a special assessment for a stated purpose and do not require all of the money collected for that stated purpose, they must return the excess to the members.

(4) On or before the date established by the benchers, each lawyer and applicant must pay to the society any special assessments set under subsection (1) (b) , unless the benchers otherwise direct.

（c）就迟延缴纳规费和摊款确定规费；

（d）确定可以全部或者部分返还规费或者摊款的情形；

（e）将律师视为在该律师未能按照主管委员认为适当的
条件支付规费或者摊款的期间内视为执业律师。

规费和摊款

24　（1）主管委员可以：

（a）确定规费，以及

（b）确定律师和申请人为律师协会目的而交纳的特别摊
款，并确定它们必须交纳的期日。

（c）［废止 2012-16-14.］

（2）［废止 2012-16-14.］

（3）如果主管委员为说明的目的设定了特别摊款，但是并不
需要为该说明的目的而征收的全部资金，则他们必须将
多余部分退还会员。

（4）在主管委员确定的期日及以前，每个律师和申请人必须
向律师协会交纳根据（1）（b）确定的任何特别摊款，除
非主管委员另有指示。

Failure to pay fee or penalty

25 (1) If a lawyer fails to pay the annual fee or a special assessment as required under this Act by the time that it is required to be paid, the lawyer ceases to be a member, unless the benchers otherwise direct, subject to rules made under section 23 (7) .

(2) The benchers may make rules providing for the suspension of a lawyer who fails to pay a fine, costs or a penalty by the time payment is required.

未能支付规费或者罚金

25　（1）在遵守根据 23（7）制定的规则的情况下，如果律师未能按照本法要求的时间交纳年度规费或者特别摊款，律师停止成为会员，除非主管委员另有指示。

（2）主管委员可以制定规则规定，对未能按照要求的时间交纳罚款、成本或者罚金的律师停止执业。

Part 3   Protection of the Public

Complaints from the public

26 (1) A person who believes that a lawyer, former lawyer or articled student has practised law incompetently or been guilty of professional misconduct, conduct unbecoming a lawyer or a breach of this Act or the rules may make a complaint to the society.

(2) The benchers may make rules authorizing an investigation into the conduct of a law firm or the conduct or competence of a lawyer, former lawyer or articled student, whether or not a complaint has been received under subsection (1).

(3) For the purposes of subsection (4), the benchers may designate an employee of the society or appoint a practising lawyer or a person whose qualifications are satisfactory to the benchers.

(4) For the purposes of an investigation authorized by rules made under subsection (2), an employee designated or a person appointed under subsection (3) may make an order requiring a person to do either or both of the following:

(a) attend, in person or by electronic means, before the

第 3 节　保护公众

公众投诉

26　（1）一个人如果认为律师、前律师或者见习生的法律执业活动不称职、有职业不端行为、与律师身份不相适的行为或者违反了本法或者规则，可以向律师协会提出投诉。

　　（2）主管委员可以制定规则，授权调查律师事务所的行为，或者律师、前律师或者见习生的行为或者称职性，无论是否根据（1）收到了投诉。

　　（3）就（4）之目的而言，主管委员可以指派律师协会的雇员或者任命执业律师或者其资格令主管委员满意的人员。

　　（4）为了进行根据（2）制定的规则所授权进行的调查之目的，根据（3）指派的雇员或者任命的人员可以作出命令，要求某人从事下列活动之一或者二者：

　　（a）亲自或者以电子方式到指派的雇员或者任命的人员面

designated employee or appointed person to answer questions on oath or affirmation, or in any other manner;

(b) produce for the designated employee or appointed person a record or thing in the person's possession or control.

(5) The society may apply to the Supreme Court for an order:

(a) directing a person to comply with an order made under subsection (4) , or

(b) directing an officer or governing member of a person to cause the person to comply with an order made under subsection (4) .

(6) The failure or refusal of a person subject to an order under subsection (4) to makes the person, on application to the Supreme Court by the society, liable to be committed for contempt as if in breach of an order or judgment of the Supreme Court:

(a) attend before the designated employee or appointed person,

(b) take an oath or make an affirmation,

(c) answer questions, or

(d) produce records or things in the person's possession or control.

Suspension during investigation

26.01 (1) The benchers may make rules permitting 3 or more

前，以宣誓、郑重声明或者任何其他方式回答询问；

（b）向指派的雇员或者任命的人员出示该人持有或者控
制的记录或者物品。

（5）律师协会可以向最高法院申请下列命令：

（a）指令一个人遵守根据（4）作出的命令，或者

（b）指令该人的职员或者管理成员敦促该人遵守根据（4）
作出的命令。

（6）一个人未能或者拒绝遵守根据（4）作出的关于下列事项
的命令，经律师协会向最高法院申请，将使该人像违反
最高法院的命令或者判决那样承担藐视法庭的责任：

（a）到指派的雇员或者任命的人员面前，

（b）宣示或者郑重声明，

（c）回答问题，或者

（d）出示该人持有或者控制的记录或者物品。

在调查期间停止执业

26.01　（1）主管委员可以制定规则，允许 3 个或者 3 个以上主管

benchers to make the following orders during an investigation, if those benchers are satisfied it is necessary to protect the public:

(a) suspend a lawyer who is the subject of the investigation;

(b) impose conditions or limitations on the practice of a lawyer who is the subject of the investigation;

(c) suspend the enrolment of an articled student who is the subject of the investigation;

(d) impose conditions or limitations on the enrolment of an articled student who is the subject of the investigation.

(2) Rules made under subsection (1) must

(a) provide for a proceeding to take place before an order is made,

(b) set out the term of a suspension, condition or limitation, and

(c) provide for review of an order made under subsection (1) and for confirmation, variation or rescission of the order.

(3) Rules made under this section and section 26.02 may provide for practice and procedure for a matter referred to in subsection (2) (a) and (c) or section 26.02 (3) and may specify that some or all practices and procedures in those proceedings may be determined by the benchers who are present at the proceeding.

委员在调查期间，在其确信有必要保护公众的情况下，作
出下列命令：

（a）被调查的律师停止执业；

（b）就被调查的律师的执业活动设定条件或者限制；

（c）停止被调查的见习生的注册；

（d）就被调查的见习生的注册设定条件或者限制。

（2）根据（1）制定的规则必须：

（a）规定作出命令之前发生的程序，

（b）列明停止执业的条款、条件或者限制，以及

（c）规定对根据（1）作出的命令进行审查，以及该
命令的维持、变更或者撤销。

（3）根据本条和 26.02 制定的规则，可以就（2）（a）和
（c）或者 26.02（3）所称事项规定操作和程序，可以
具体规定这些程序中的某些或者全部操作和程序可以
由出席该程序的主管委员确定。

Medical examination

26.02 (1) The benchers may make rules permitting 3 or more benchers to make an order requiring a lawyer or an articled student to

  (a) submit to an examination by a medical practitioner specified by the benchers, and

  (b) instruct the medical practitioner to report to the benchers on the ability of the lawyer to practise law or, in the case of an articled student, the ability of the student to complete his or her articles.

(2) Before making an order under subsection (1), the benchers making the order must be of the opinion that the order is likely necessary to protect the public.

(3) Rules made under subsection (1) must

  (a) provide for a proceeding to take place before an order is made, and

  (b) provide for review of an order under subsection (1) and for confirmation, variation or rescission of the order.

Written notification to chief judge

26.1 If an investigation is conducted in accordance with the rules established under section 26 (2) of this Act respecting a lawyer or former lawyer who is also a "part time judicial justice", as that term is defined in section 1 of the Provincial

医学检查

26.02 （1）主管委员可以制定规则，允许 3 个或者 3 个以上的主
　　　　管委员作出命令，要求律师或者见习生：

　　　　　　（a）接受主管委员具体指定的执业医师的检查，以及

　　　　　　（b）指示执业医师就律师从事法律执业活动或者见习
　　　　　　　　生完成其见习的能力，向主管委员作出报告。

　　　　（2）在根据（1）作出命令之前，作出命令的主管委员必
　　　　　　须认为该命令有可能为保护公众所必需。

　　　　（3）根据（1）制定的规则必须：
　　　　　　（a）规定在作出命令之前发生的程序，以及

　　　　　　（b）规定对根据（1）作出的命令进行审查，以及该
　　　　　　　　命令的维持、变更或者撤销。

向首席法官发出书面通知

26.1　如果正在遵照根据本法 26（2）确立的规则对也是"兼职法
　　　　官"（该术语的定义见《省法院法》第 1 条）的律师或者前
　　　　律师进行调查，律师协会必须尽可能早地向根据《省法院
　　　　法》第 10 条指派的首席法官提供包括下列信息的书面通知：

Court Act, the society must, as soon as practicable, provide a written notification to the chief judge designated under section 10 of the Provincial Court Act that includes the following information:

(a) the name of the lawyer or former lawyer;

(b) confirmation that an investigation is being conducted with respect to that lawyer or former lawyer.

Practice standards

27 (1) The benchers may

(a) set standards of practice for lawyers,

(b) establish and maintain a program to assist lawyers in handling or avoiding personal, emotional, medical or substance abuse problems, and

(c) establish and maintain a program to assist lawyers on issues arising from the practice of law.

(2) The benchers may make rules to do any of the following:

(a) establish a practice standards committee and delegate any or all authority and responsibility under this section, other than rule-making authority, to that committee;

(b) permit an investigation into a lawyer's competence to practise law if

(i) there are reasonable grounds to believe that the lawyer is practising law in an incompetent manner, or

(ii) the lawyer consents;

（a）律师或者前律师的姓名；

（b）确认正在就律师或者前律师进行调查。

执业标准

27　（1）主管委员可以：

　　（a）设定律师执业标准，

　　（b）建立和维护帮助律师处理或者避免人身、情感、医学或者药物滥用问题的计划，以及

　　（c）建立和维护帮助律师处理法律执业活动中产生的问题的计划。

（2）主管委员可以就任何下列事项制定规则：

　　（a）建立执业标准委员会，并将本条规定的任何或者全部权力和责任委派给该委员会，制定规则的权力除外；

　　（b）在下列情况下，允许调查律师从事法律执业活动的称职性：

　　　（i）有合理根据认为律师在以不称职的方式从事法律执业活动，或者

　　　（ii）律师表示同意；

(c) require a lawyer whose competence to practise law is under investigation to answer questions and provide access to information, files or records in the lawyer's possession or control;

(d) provide for a report to the benchers of the findings of an investigation into the competence of a lawyer to practise law;

(d.1) permit the practice standards committee established under paragraph (a) to make orders imposing conditions and limitations on lawyers' practices, and to require lawyers whose competence to practise law has been investigated to comply with those orders;

(e) permit the benchers to order that a lawyer, a former lawyer, an articled student or a law firm pay to the society the costs of an investigation or remedial program under this Part and set and extend the time for payment;

(f) permit the discipline committee established under section 36 (a) to consider

(i) the findings of an investigation into a lawyer's competence to practise law,

(ii) any remedial program undertaken or recommended,

(iii) any order that imposes conditions or limitations on the practice of a lawyer, and

(iv) any failure to comply with an order that imposes conditions or limitations on the practice of a lawyer.

（c）要求其从事法律执业活动的称职性受到调查的律师回答问题并提供对律师所持有或者控制的信息、卷宗或者记录的近用；

（d）就律师从事法律执业活动的称职性的调查结果向主管委员提供报告；

（d.1）允许根据（a）建立的执业标准委员会作出命令，来就律师的执业活动设定条件和限制，并要求其从事法律执业活动的称职性受到调查的律师遵守这些命令；

（e）允许主管委员命令律师、前律师、见习生或者律师事务所向律师协会交纳根据本节进行的调查或者补救计划的成本，并确定和延长交纳的时间；

（f）允许根据 36（a）建立的惩戒委员会审议：

（i）对律师从事法律执业活动的称职性进行调查的结果，

（ii）任何采取或者建议的补救程序，

（iii）就律师的执业活动设定条件或者限制的任何命令，以及

（iv）未能遵守就律师的执业活动设定的条件或者限制的行为。

(3) The amount of costs ordered to be paid by a person under the rules made under subsection (2) (e) may be recovered as a debt owing to the society and, when collected, the amount is the property of the society.

(3.1) For the purpose of recovering a debt under subsection (3), the executive director may

(a) issue a certificate stating that the amount of costs is due, the amount remaining unpaid, including interest, and the name of the person required to pay it, and

(b) file the certificate with the Supreme Court.

(3.2) A certificate filed under subsection (3.1) with the Supreme Court is of the same effect, and proceedings may be taken on it, as if it were a judgment of the Supreme Court for the recovery of a debt in the amount stated against the person named in it.

(4) Rules made under subsection (2) (d.1)

(a) may include rules respecting

(i) the making of orders by the practice standards committee, and

(ii) the conditions and limitations that may be imposed on the practice of a lawyer, and

(b) must not permit the imposition of conditions or limitations on the practice of a lawyer before the lawyer has been notified of the reasons for the proposed order and given a reasonable opportunity to make representations respecting those reasons.

（3）根据依（2）（e）制定的规则命令由某人支付的成本，可
　　以作为对律师协会的债务进行追讨，在追回后，该款项
　　是律师协会的财产。

（3.1）为根据（3）追回债务，执行主任可以：

　　（a）签发证明，说明所欠成本的数额、仍然未付的数额，
　　　　包括利息，以及需要支付这些款额的人员的姓名，
　　　　以及

　　（b）将该证明提交最高法院存档。

（3.2）根据（3.1）向最高法院存档的证明，与最高法院作出的
　　　向其列名者追讨所载数额的债务的判决具有同等效力，
　　　可以据此提起程序。

（4）根据（2）（d.1）制定的规则：

　　（a）可以包括关于下列事项的规则：

　　　　（i）由执业标准委员会作出命令，以及

　　　　（ii）就律师的执业活动可以设定的条件和限制，以及

　　（b）在就准备作出的命令的理由通知律师，并给其以合
　　　　理机会来就这些理由作出解释之前，不得允许就律
　　　　师的执业活动设定条件或者限制。

Education

28   The benchers may take any steps they consider advisable to promote and improve the standard of practice by lawyers, including but not limited to the following:

  (a) establishing and maintaining or otherwise supporting a system of legal education, including but not limited to the following programs:

   (i) professional legal training;

   (ii) continuing legal education;

   (iii) remedial legal education;

   (iv) loss prevention;

  (b) granting scholarships, bursaries and loans to persons engaged in a program of legal education;

  (c) providing funds of the society and other assistance to establish or maintain law libraries in British Columbia;

  (d) providing for publication of court and other legal decisions and legal resource materials.

Specialization and restricted practice

29   The benchers may make rules to do any of the following:

  (a) provide for the manner and extent to which lawyers or law firms may hold themselves out as engaging in restricted or preferred areas of practice;

  (b) provide for the qualification and certification of lawyers as specialists in areas of practice designated under paragraph(c);

教育

28 主管委员可以采取其认为可取的措施，促进和提高律师执业活动的标准，包括但是不限于下列事项：

（a）建立和维持或者以其他方式支持法律教育制度，包括但是不限于下列计划：

（i）法律职业培训；

（ii）法律继续教育；

（iii）补救性法律教育；

（iv）损失防范；

（b）对参加法律教育计划的人员提供奖学金、助学金和贷款；

（c）提供律师协会的资金和其他帮助，在不列颠哥伦比亚建立或者维持法律图书馆；

（d）提供法院出版物和其他法律决定和法律渊源材料。

专业化和限定执业领域

29 主管委员可以制定规则从事下列活动：

（a）规定律师或者律师事务所可以宣示自己从事限定的或者优选的执业领域的方式和范围；

（b）规定律师作为根据（c）定名的执业领域的专家的资格和证书；

(c) designate specialized areas of practice and provide that lawyers must not hold themselves out as restricting their practices to, preferring or specializing in a designated area of practice unless the lawyer has met the qualifications required for certification under a rule made under paragraph (b) ;

(d) establish qualifications for and conditions under which practising lawyers may practise as mediators.

Insurance

30 (1) In this section, "trust protection insurance" means insurance for lawyers to compensate persons who suffer pecuniary loss as a result of dishonest appropriation of money or other property entrusted to and received by a lawyer in his or her capacity as a barrister and solicitor.

(1.1) The benchers must make rules requiring lawyers to maintain professional liability and trust protection insurance.

(2) The benchers may establish, administer, maintain and operate a professional liability insurance program and may use for that purpose fees set under this section.

(2.1) The benchers

(a) must establish, administer, maintain and operate a trust protection insurance program and may use for that purpose fees set under this section,

(b) may establish conditions and qualifications for a claim against a lawyer under the trust protection insurance

（c）就专业化执业领域定名，并规定律师不得宣示自己将其执业活动首选为或者专门从事定名的业务领域，除非律师已经达到了根据依（b）制定的规则规定的证书所要求的资格；

（d）确立执业律师可以作为调解人执业的资格和条件。

保险

30　（1）在本条中，"信托保护保险"是指为赔偿因律师不诚实地挪用信托给出庭律师和事务律师身份的律师或者该律师收到的资金或者其他财产而遭受经济损失的人员的保险。

（1.1）主管委员必须制定规则，要求律师保持职业责任和信托保护保险。

（2）主管委员可以建立、管理、维护和运营职业责任保险计划，并可以为该目的使用根据本条确定的规费。

（2.1）主管委员：

（a）必须建立、管理、维护和运营信托保护保险计划，并可以为该目的使用根据本条确定的规费，

（b）可以就针对信托保护保险计划下的律师提出的索赔设立条件和资格，包括提出索赔的时限，以及

program, including time limitations for making a claim, and

(c) may place limitations on the amounts that may be paid out of the insurance fund established under subsection (6) in respect of a claim against a lawyer under the trust protection insurance program.

(3) The benchers may, by resolution, set

(a) the insurance fee, and

(b) the amount to be paid for each class of transaction under subsection (4)(c).

(4) The benchers may make rules to do any of the following:

(a) permit lawyers to pay the insurance fee by instalments on or before the date by which each instalment of that fee is due;

(b) establish classes of membership for insurance purposes and exempt a class of lawyers from the requirement to maintain professional liability or trust protection insurance or from payment of all or part of the insurance fee;

(c) designate classes of transactions for which a lawyer must pay a fee to fund the professional liability or trust protection insurance program.

(5) The benchers may use fees set under this section to act as the agent for the members in obtaining professional liability or trust protection insurance.

(6) The benchers must establish an insurance fund, comprising fees set under this section and other income of the professional liability and trust protection insurance programs, and the fund

（c）就针对信托保护保险计划下的律师提出的索赔，可以就从根据（6）设立的保险基金赔付的数额设定限额。

（3）主管委员可以通过决议，确定：

（a）保险费，以及

（b）根据（4）（c）对每类交易赔付的数额。

（4）主管委员可以就任何下列事项制定规则：

（a）允许律师在分期付款期日或者之前，分期支付保险费；

（b）为保险目的建立会员类别，对某律师类别免除保持职业责任或者信托保护保险的要求，或者免交全部或者部分保险费；

（c）确定律师必须付费来资助职业责任或者信托保护保险计划的交易类别。

（5）主管委员可以使用根据本条确定的规费，充任会员的代理人，来获得职业责任或者信托保护保险。

（6）主管委员必须建立保险基金，该基金由根据本条设定的规费和职业责任和信托保护保险计划的其他收入构成，并且该基金：

(a) must be accounted for separately from other funds,

(b) is not subject to any process of seizure or attachment by a creditor of the society, and

(c) is not subject to a trust in favour of a person who has sustained a loss.

(7) Subject to rules made under section 23 (7) , a lawyer must not practise law unless the lawyer has paid the insurance fee when it is due, or is exempted from payment of the fee.

(8) A lawyer must immediately surrender to the executive director his or her practising certificate and any proof of professional liability or trust protection insurance issued by the society, if

(a) the society has, on behalf of the lawyer,

(i) paid a deductible amount under the professional liability insurance program in respect of a claim or potential claim under that program, or

(ii) made an indemnity payment under the trust protection insurance program in respect of a claim under that program, and

(b) the lawyer has not reimbursed the society at the date that the insurance fee or an instalment of that fee is due.

(9) The benchers may waive or extend the time

(a) to pay all or part of the insurance fee, or

(b) to repay all or part of a deductible amount paid under the professional liability insurance program or an indemnity payment made under the trust protection insurance program on behalf of a lawyer.

（a）必须与其他基金独立结算，

（b）不受律师协会债权人的任何查封和扣押，以及

（c）不受到有利于已经遭受损失的人员的信托。

（7）在遵守根据 23（7）制定的规则的情况下，律师不得从事
　　法律执业活动，除非律师已经缴纳了所欠保险费，或者
　　被免于缴纳该保险费。

（8）在下列情况下，律师必须立即向执行主任上交其执业证
　　书和律师协会签发的关于职业责任或者信托保护保险的
　　任何证明：

　　（a）律师协会已经代表律师，

　　　　（i）就职业责任保险计划规定的索赔或者潜在索赔，
　　　　　　支付了该计划规定的免赔额，或者

　　　　（ii）根据信托保护保险计划，就根据该计划提出的
　　　　　　索赔进行了赔偿，以及

　　（b）律师在保险费或者保险费分期付款到期日还没有偿
　　　　还律师协会。

（9）主管委员可以放弃下列付款或者延长其时间：

　　（a）支付全部或者部分保险费，或者

　　（b）偿还代表律师支付的全部或者部分职业责任保险计
　　　　划免赔额或者根据信托保护保险计划进行的赔偿。

(10) If the benchers extend the time for a payment under subsection (9) , the later date for payment is the date when payment is due for the purposes of subsections (7) and (8) .

(11) A payment made from the insurance fund established under subsection (6) in respect of a claim against a lawyer under the trust protection insurance program

(a) may be recovered from the lawyer or former lawyer on whose account it was paid, or from the estate of that person, as a debt owing to the society, and

(b) if collected, is the property of the society and must be accounted for as part of the fund.

Repealed

31 [Repealed 2012-16-20.]

Financial responsibility

32 (1) The benchers may establish standards of financial responsibility relating to the integrity and financial viability of the professional practice of a lawyer or law firm.

(2) The benchers may make rules to do any of the following:

(a) provide for the examination of the books, records and accounts of lawyers and law firms and the answering of questions by lawyers and representatives of law firms to determine whether standards established under this

（10）如果主管委员根据（9）延长了付款时间，就（7）和
　　　（8）目的而言，较迟的付款期日是付款到期日。

（11）就根据信托保护保险计划对律师提出的索赔而从根据
　　　（6）设立的保险基金中所付款项：

　　（a）作为对律师协会的债务，可以从为其缘故而付款的
　　　　　律师或者前律师那里追讨，或者从该人的遗产中追
　　　　　讨，以及
　　（b）在追回后，是律师协会的财产，必须作为基金的一
　　　　　部分结算。

废止

31　［废止 2012-16-20.］

经济责任

32　（1）主管委员可以就律师或者律师事务所的职业业务活动的
　　　　适正性和财务可行性建立经济责任标准。

　　（2）主管委员可以就任何下列事项制定规则：
　　　　（a）规定对律师和律师事务所的账簿、记录和账户的检
　　　　　　　查，律师和律师事务所的代表对提问进行回答，以
　　　　　　　确定是否达到了根据本条建立的标准；

section are being met;

(b) permit the suspension of a lawyer who does not meet the standards established under subsection (1);

(c) permit the imposition of conditions and limitations on a law firm that, or the practice of a lawyer who, does not meet the standards established under subsection (1).

(3) Rules made under subsection (2)(b) and (c) must not permit the suspension of a lawyer or imposition of conditions and limitations on the practice of a lawyer or the imposition of conditions and limitations on a law firm before the lawyer or law firm, as the case may be, has been notified of the reasons for the proposed action and given a reasonable opportunity to make representations respecting those reasons.

Trust accounts

33 (1) The benchers may require a lawyer or law firm to do any of the following:

(a) provide information or an annual report concerning the lawyer's or law firm's books and accounts;

(b) have all or part of the lawyer's or law firm's books and accounts audited or reviewed annually;

(c) provide the executive director with an accountant's report on the lawyer's or law firm's books and accounts.

(2) The benchers may

(a) exempt classes of lawyers or law firms from some or all of the requirements of subsection (1), and

（b）允许对没有达到根据（1）建立的标准的律师停止
　　执业；

（c）允许对没有达到根据（1）建立的标准的律师事务所
　　或者律师的执业活动设定条件和限制。

（3）根据（2）（b）和（c）制定的规则，在就准备采取的行
　　动的理由对律师和律师事务所（视情况而定）进行通知，
　　并给其以合理机会就这些理由作出说明之前，不得允许
　　对律师处以停止执业或者就律师的业务活动设定条件和
　　限制，或者对律师事务所设定条件和限制。

信托账户

33　（1）主管委员可以要求律师或者律师事务所从事任何下列活动：

（a）就律师或者律师事务所的账簿和账户提供信息和年
　　度报告；

（b）就律师或者律师事务所的全部或者部分账簿和账户
　　进行年度审计或者审查；

（c）向执行主任提供会计师关于律师或者律师事务所账
　　簿和账户的报告。

（2）主管委员可以：

（a）对律师或者律师事务所类别，免除某些或者全部（1）
　　规定要求，以及

(b) determine the qualifications required of a person performing an audit or review referred to in subsection (1).

(3) The benchers may make rules to do any of the following:

(a) establish standards of accounting for and management of funds held in trust by lawyers or law firms;

(b) designate savings institutions and classes of savings institutions in which lawyers or law firms may deposit money that they hold in trust;

(c) provide for precautions to be taken by lawyers and law firms for the care of funds or property held in trust by them.

(4) The rules referred to in subsection (3) apply despite section 19 of the Trustee Act.

(5) The rules made under subsection (3) may be different for

(a) lawyers and law firms, or

(b) different classes of lawyers or law firms.

Unclaimed trust money

34 (1) A lawyer who has held money in trust on behalf of a person whom the lawyer has been unable to locate for 2 years may pay the money to the society.

(2) On paying money to the society under subsection (1), the liability of the lawyer to pay that money to the person on whose behalf it was held or to that person's legal representative is extinguished.

(3) The society must hold in trust any money paid to it under

（b）确定进行（1）所称的审计或者审查的人员所需要具
备的资格。

（3）主管委员可以就任何下列事项制定规则：

（a）就律师或者律师事务所信托持有的资金的结算和管
理建立标准；

（b）指定律师或者律师事务所可以储蓄其信托持有的储
蓄机构和储蓄机构的类别；

（c）规定律师和律师事务所就关照其信托持有的资金或
者财产所要采取的防范措施。

（4）尽管有《受托人法》第 19 条之规定，（3）所称规则也适用。

（5）根据（3）制定的规则，可以就下列主题有所不同：

（a）律师和律师事务所，或者

（b）不同的律师或者律师事务所类别。

无人领取的信托资金

34　（1）如果律师为某人信托持有资金，但是在 2 年内律师不能
找到该人，律师可以将该资金付给律师协会。

（2）在根据（1）将代表某人持有的资金付给律师协会时，律
师向该人或者该人的法律代表支付该资金的责任被消灭。

（3）律师协会必须信托持有根据（1）支付给它的资金。

subsection (1) .

(4) The society is entitled to retain, for its purposes, interest on any money held by it under subsection (3) .

(5) A person or the person's legal representative who, but for subsections (1) and (2) , could have claimed money held by a lawyer may claim the money from the society.

(6) On being satisfied that the person claiming money under subsection (5) is entitled to it, the society must pay the money to that person together with interest on it at a rate that the benchers consider reflects market rates during the time the society held the money.

(7) If the money is not paid out under subsection (6) within 5 years after its receipt by the society under subsection (1) , the society must pay the money, excluding any interest retained under subsection (4) , to the foundation for its purposes, but subsections (5) and (6) continue to apply as though the money had not been paid to the foundation.

(8) The foundation must indemnify the society for any claims paid under subsection (6) in respect of money received from the society under subsection (7) , including interest paid by the society under subsection (6) for the period when the money was held by the foundation.

(9) A person whose claim against the society under subsection (5) has been refused may apply to the Supreme Court for a review of the decision of the society.

(10) On a claim under subsection (9) , the court may allow the claim plus interest in an amount determined by it.

（4）律师协会有权为其目的保留根据（3）持有的任何资金的
　　利息。

（5）除了（1）和（2）外，本可以就律师持有的资金提出主张的
　　人员或者该人的法律代表，可以向律师协会主张该资金。

（6）在确信根据（5）主张资金的人员有权得到该资金时，律
　　师协会必须将该资金及其主管委员认为反映了律师协会
　　持有该资金期间的市场利率的利息支付给该人。

（7）如果律师协会在根据（1）收到资金后 5 年内没有根据
　　（6）将该资金付出，律师协会必须在扣除根据（4）保有
　　的任何利息后，将该资金支付给基金会用于其目的，但
　　是（5）和（6）继续适用，就像该资金没有支付给基金
　　会那样。

（8）基金会必须补偿律师协会针对任何主张根据（6）就其根
　　据（7）接受的资金所付的款项，包括律师协会根据（6）
　　就基金会持有资金的期间所支付的利息。

（9）根据（5）向律师协会索赔但是被拒绝的人员，可以向最
　　高法院申请对律师协会的决定进行审查。

（10）就根据（9）提出的主张，法院可以允许索赔加上利息，
　　　其数额由法院决定。

(11) The benchers may make rules to do any of the following:

(a) create and maintain a fund consisting of money paid to the society under subsection (1) ;

(b) establish procedures for investigating and adjudicating claims made under subsection (5) .

(12) [Repealed 1999-48-28.]

Restriction on suspended and disbarred lawyers

35 On application of the society, the Supreme Court may order that a person referred to in section 15 (3) (a) or (b) be prohibited from acting as any or all of the following until the person is a member in good standing of the society or until the court orders otherwise:

(a) a personal representative of a deceased person;

(b) a trustee of the estate of a deceased person;

(c) a committee under the Patients Property Act;

(c.1) an attorney under Part 2 of the Power of Attorney Act;

(d) a representative under the Representation Agreement Act.

（11）主管委员可以就任何下列事项制定规则：

  （a）创建和维护由根据（1）支付给律师协会的资金构成的基金；

  （b）就调查和裁决根据（5）提出的主张建立程序。

（12）［废止 1999-48-28.］

对被停止执业和取消律师资格的律师的限制

35 根据律师协会的申请，最高法院可以命令 15（3）（a）或者（b）所称人员被禁止担任下列任何或者全部角色，直至该人成为律师协会资格完好的会员，或者直至法院另有命令：

（a）已故人员的个人代表；

（b）已故人员的遗产受托人；

（c）《患者财产法》规定的委员会；

（c.1）《授权委托法》第 2 节规定的律师；

（d）《代理协议法》规定的代表。

Part 4 Discipline

Discipline rules

36 The benchers may make rules to do any of the following:

   (a) establish a discipline committee and delegate any or all authority and responsibility under this Part, other than rule-making authority, to that committee;

   (b) authorize an investigation of the books, records and accounts of a lawyer if there is reason to believe that the lawyer may have committed any misconduct, conduct unbecoming a lawyer or a breach of this Act or the rules;

   (c) authorize an examination of the books, records and accounts of a lawyer or law firm;

   (d) require a lawyer or law firm to cooperate with an investigation or examination under paragraph (b) or (c), including producing records and other evidence and providing explanations on request;

   (e) require a lawyer or articled student to appear before the benchers, a committee or other body to discuss the conduct or competence of the lawyer or articled student;

   (e.1) require a representative of a law firm to appear before the

第 4 节　惩戒

惩戒规则

36　主管委员可以就任何下列事项制定规则：

（a）建立惩戒委员会，并将本节规定的任何或者全部权力和
责任委派给该委员会，规则制定权除外；

（b）在有理由认为律师可能实施了任何不端行为、与律师身
份不相称的行为或者违反了本法或者规则的情况下，授
权调查该律师的账簿、记录和账户；

（c）授权检查律师或者律师事务所的账簿、记录和账户；

（d）要求律师或者律师事务所配合根据（b）或者（c）进行
的调查和检查，包括出示记录和其他证据，并经要求作
出解释；

（e）要求律师或者见习生在主管委员、委员会或者其他组织
前到场，讨论律师或者见习生的行为或者称职性；

（e.1）要求律师事务所的代表在主管委员、委员会或者其他组

benchers, a committee or other body to discuss the conduct of the law firm;

(f) authorize the ordering of a hearing into the conduct or competence of a lawyer or an articled student, or the conduct of a law firm, by issuing a citation;

(g) authorize the rescission of a citation;

(h) permit the benchers to summarily suspend or disbar a lawyer convicted of an offence that was proceeded with by way of indictment or convicted in another jurisdiction of an offence that, in the opinion of the benchers, is equivalent to an offence that may be proceeded with by way of indictment;

(i) establish a process for the protection of the privacy and the severing, destruction or return of personal, business or other records that are unrelated to an investigation or examination and that, in error or incidentally, form part of

(i) the books, records or accounts of a lawyer, an articled student or a law firm authorized to be investigated or examined under a rule made under paragraph (b) or section 26, or

(ii) files or other records that are seized in accordance with an order of the Supreme Court under section 37.

Search and seizure

37 (1) The society may apply to the Supreme Court for an order that the files or other records, wherever located, of or relating to a lawyer or articled student be seized from the

织前到场，讨论律师事务所的行为；

（f）通过签发传唤证，授权命令就律师或者见习生的行为或者称职性、律师事务所的行为举行听证；

（g）授权撤销传唤证；

（h）对于经公诉被判定有罪的律师或者在其他司法辖区被判定有罪，且在主管委员看来相当于可以通过公诉处理的犯罪，允许主管委员速决停止执业或者取消律师资格；

（i）建立程序，以保护隐私，以及区分、销毁或者退还与调查或者检查无关，错误或者附带成为下列材料的一部分的个人、商业或者其他记录：

（i）根据依（b）或者第 26 条制定的规则，被调查或者检查的律师、见习生或者律师事务所账簿、记录或者账户，或者

（ii）遵照最高法院根据第 37 条作出的命令扣押的卷宗或者其他记录。

搜查和扣押

37 （1）如果有合理根据认为律师或者见习生可能实施了或者将会实施任何下列行为，律师协会可以向最高法院申请命令，要求从命令上列名的人员那里扣押律师或者见习生

person named in the order, if there are reasonable grounds to believe that a lawyer or articled student may have committed or will commit any

(a) misconduct,

(b) conduct unbecoming a lawyer, or

(c) breach of this Act or the rules.

(2) An application under subsection (1) may be made without notice to anyone or on such notice as the judge requires.

(3) If the application under subsection (1) is in relation to the conduct of an articled student, the order may be made in respect of the books, accounts, files or other records of the student's principal or the principal's firm.

(4) In an application under subsection (1) , the person making the application must state on oath or affirmation the grounds for believing the matter referred to in subsection(1) and the grounds for believing that the seizure will produce evidence relevant to that matter.

(5) In an order under subsection (1) , the court may

(a) designate the person who will conduct the seizure and authorize that person to conduct it,

(b) state the time and place where the seizure will take place, and

(c) give any other directions that are necessary to carry out the seizure.

的或者与之有关的卷宗或者其他记录（无论在哪里）：

（a）不端行为，

（b）与律师身份不相称的行为，或者

（c）违反本法或者规则的行为。

（2）根据（1）提出的申请，可以不通知任何人或者遵照法官的要求进行通知。

（3）如果根据（1）提出的申请与见习生的行为有关，可以就该见习生的负责人或者负责人的律师事务所的账簿、卷宗或者其他记录作出命令。

（4）在根据（1）提出的申请中，提出申请的人必须经过宣誓或者郑重声明，说明认为（1）所称事项和认为扣押将会产生与该事项有关的证据的理由。

（5）在根据（1）作出的命令中，法院可以：

（a）指派进行扣押的人员，并授权该人进行扣押，

（b）说明进行扣押的时间和地点，以及

（c）作出为执行扣押所必需的任何其他指令。

Personal records in investigation or seizure

37.1 In conducting an investigation or examination of books, records or accounts under section 26 or rules made under section 36 (b) or in the seizure of files or other records in accordance with an order of the Supreme Court under section 37, the society may collect personal information unrelated to the investigation or examination that, in error or incidentally, is contained in those books, accounts, files or records, but the society must, subject to rules made under section 36 (i) :

(a) return that personal information if and as soon as practicable, or

(b) destroy that personal information.

Discipline hearings

38 (1) This section applies to the hearing of a citation.

(2) A hearing must be conducted before a panel.

(3) A panel must

(a) make a determination and take action according to this section,

(b) give written reasons for its determination about the conduct or competence of the respondent and any action taken against the respondent, and

(c) record in writing any order for costs.

(4) After a hearing, a panel must do one of the following:

(a) dismiss the citation;

调查或者扣押的个人记录

37.1 在根据第 26 条或者根据 36（b）制定的规则对账簿、记录或者账户进行调查或者检查时，或者在遵照最高法院根据第 37 条作出的命令对卷宗或者其他记录进行扣押时，律师协会可以收集错误或者附带包含在这些账簿、账户、卷宗或者记录中与调查或者检查无关的个人信息，但是律师协会在遵守根据 36（i）制定的规则的情况下，必须：

（a）在可行的情况下尽可能早地归还该个人信息，或者

（b）销毁该个人信息。

惩戒听证

38 （1）本条适用于关于传唤证的听证。

（2）听证必须由专责小组进行。

（3）专责小组必须：

（a）根据本条作出决定并采取行动，

（b）就其关于应诉人的行为或者称职性的决定以及对应诉人采取的行动，给出书面理由，以及

（c）以书面形式记录关于成本的任何命令。

（4）在听证后，专责小组必须采取下列措施之一：

（a）驳回传唤证；

(b) determine that the respondent has committed one or more of the following:

(i) professional misconduct;

(ii) conduct unbecoming a lawyer;

(iii) a breach of this Act or the rules;

(iv) incompetent performance of duties undertaken in the capacity of a lawyer;

(v) if the respondent is not a member, conduct that would, if the respondent were a member, constitute professional misconduct, conduct unbecoming a lawyer, or a breach of this Act or the rules;

(c) [Repealed 2012-16-27.]

(5) If an adverse determination is made against a respondent, other than an articled student, under subsection (4) , the panel must do one or more of the following:

(a) reprimand the respondent;

(b) fine the respondent an amount not exceeding $50 000;

(c) impose conditions or limitations on the respondent's practice;

(d) suspend the respondent from the practice of law or from practice in one or more fields of law

(i) for a specified period of time,

(ii) until the respondent fulfills a condition imposed under paragraph (c) or subsection (7) or complies with a requirement under paragraph (f) of this subsection,

(iii) from a specified date until the respondent fulfills

（b）确定应诉人实施了下列一个或者多个行为：

（i）职业不端行为；

（ii）与律师身份不相称的行为；

（iii）违反本法或者规则的行为；

（iv）不称职地履行以律师身份承担的职责；

（v）如果应诉人不是会员，在该人是会员的情况下，
将构成职业不端行为，与律师身份不相称的行
为，或者违反本法或者规则之行为的行为；

（c）［废止 2012-16-27.］

（5）如果根据（4）对见习生之外的应诉人作出了不利决定，
专责小组必须处以下列一个或者多个处罚：

（a）对应诉人进行申饬；

（b）对应诉人处以不超过 50 000 加元的罚款；

（c）就应诉人的执业活动设定条件或者限制；

（d）在下列期间或者条件下，停止应诉人的法律执业活
动或者在一个或者多个法律领域的执业活动：

（i）具体的期间，

（ii）直至应诉人实现了根据（c）或者（7）设定的
条件，或者遵守了本款（f）规定的要求，

（iii）从某个具体期日开始，直至应诉人实现了根据

a condition imposed under paragraph (c) or subsection (7) or complies with a requirement under paragraph (f) of this subsection, or

(iv) for a specified minimum period of time and until the respondent fulfills a condition imposed under paragraph (c) or subsection (7) or complies with a requirement under paragraph (f) of this subsection;

(e) disbar the respondent;

(f) require the respondent to do one or more of the following:

(i) complete a remedial program to the satisfaction of the practice standards committee;

(ii) appear before a board of examiners appointed by the panel or by the practice standards committee and satisfy the board that the respondent is competent to practise law or to practise in one or more fields of law;

(iii) appear before a board of examiners appointed by the panel or by the practice standards committee and satisfy the board that the respondent's competence to practise law is not adversely affected by a physical or mental disability, or dependency on alcohol or drugs;

(iv) practise law only as a partner, employee or associate of one or more other lawyers;

(g) prohibit a respondent who is not a member but who

（c）或者（7）设定的条件，或者遵守了本款

（f）规定的要求，或者

（iv）在具体最低期间内，且直至应诉人实现了根据

（c）或者（7）设定的条件，或者遵守了本款

（f）规定的要求；

（e）取消应诉人的律师资格；

（f）要求应诉人从事下列一个或者多个活动：

（i）令执业标准委员会满意地完成某补救计划；

（ii）在专责小组或者执业标准委员会指定的检查委

员会前到场，并使该委员会确信应诉人具有从

事法律执业活动或者在一个或者多个领域具有

从事法律执业活动的称职性；

（iii）在专责小组或者执业标准委员会指定的检查委

员会前到场，并使该委员会确信应诉人从事法

律执业活动的称职性没有受到生理或者精神失

能、酒精或者药物依赖的不利影响；

（iv）仅能作为一个或者多个其他律师的合伙人、雇

员或者非合伙人从事法律执业活动；

（g）禁止不是会员但是依照根据 16（2）（a）或者 17（1）

is permitted to practise law under a rule made under section 16 (2) (a) or 17 (1) (a) from practising law in British Columbia indefinitely or for a specified period of time.

(6) If an adverse determination is made under subsection (4) against an articled student, the panel may do one or more of the following:

(a) reprimand the articled student;

(b) fine the articled student an amount not exceeding C$5 000;

(c) extend the period that the articled student is required to serve under articles;

(d) set aside the enrolment of the articled student.

(7) In addition to its powers under subsections (5) and (6) , a panel may make any other orders and declarations and impose any conditions it considers appropriate.

(8) A fine imposed under this Act may be recovered as a debt owing to the society and, when collected, it is the property of the society.

(9) For the purpose of recovering a debt under subsection (8) , the executive director may

(a) issue a certificate stating that the fine is due, the amount remaining unpaid, including interest, and the name of the person required to pay it, and

(b) file the certificate with the Supreme Court.

(10) A certificate filed under subsection (9) with the Supreme Court is of the same effect, and proceedings may be taken

（a）制定的规则被允许从事法律执业活动的应诉人在不列颠哥伦比亚不定期或者定期从事法律执业活动。

（6）如果根据（4）对见习生作出了不利决定，专责小组可以处以下列一个或者多个处罚：

（a）对见习生进行申饬；

（b）对见习生处以不超过 5 000 加元的罚款；

（c）延长见习生需要见习的期间；

（d）搁置见习生的注册。

（7）除了（5）和（6）规定的权力外，专责小组可以作出任何其他命令和宣告，以及设定它认为适当的任何条件。

（8）根据本法处以的罚款，可以作为对律师协会的债务加以追讨，在追回后，是律师协会的财产。

（9）为追讨（8）规定的债务之目的，执行主任可以：

（a）签发证明，说明所欠罚款的数额、仍然未付的数额，包括利息，以及需要支付这些款额的人员的姓名，以及

（b）将该证明提交最高法院。

（10）根据（9）向最高法院提交的证明，与最高法院就向证明中所列人员追讨所载数额的债务所作出的判决，具有

on it, as if it were a judgment of the Supreme Court for the recovery of a debt in the amount stated against the person named in it.

Suspension

39 (1) The benchers may make rules permitting 3 or more benchers to do any of the following until the decision of a hearing panel or other disposition of the subject matter of the hearing:

(a) suspend a respondent who is an individual, if the respondent's continued practice would be dangerous to the public or the respondent's clients;

(b) impose conditions or limitations on the practice of a respondent who is an individual;

(c) suspend the enrolment of a respondent who is an articled student;

(d) impose conditions or limitations on the enrolment of a respondent who is an articled student.

(2) Rules made under subsection (1) must

(a) provide for a proceeding to take place before an order is made,

(b) set out the term of a suspension, condition or limitation, and

(c) provide for review of an order made under subsection (1) and for confirmation, variation or rescission of the order.

同等效力，可以就此提起程序。

停止执业

39 （1）主管委员可以制定规则，允许3个或者3个以上的主管委员从事任何下列活动，直至专责小组的听证作出决定或者就听证事项作出其他处置：

（a）如果作为自然人的应诉人继续执业将会给公众或者应诉人的委托人带来危险，对其停止执业；

（b）就作为自然人的应诉人的业务活动设定条件或者限制；

（c）就作为见习生的应诉人停止注册；

（d）就作为见习生的应诉人的注册设定条件或者限制。

（2）根据（1）制定的规则必须：
（a）规定在作出命令之前进行的程序，

（b）列明停止执业的条款、条件或者限制，以及

（c）就根据（1）作出的命令的审查，以及该命令的维持、变更或者撤销作出规定。

(3) Rules made under this section may provide for practice and procedure for a matter referred to in subsection (2) (a) and (c) and may specify that some or all practices and procedures in those proceedings may be determined by the benchers who are present at the proceeding.

Repealed

40 [Repealed 2012-16-29.]

（3）根据本条制定的规则可以就（2）（a）和（c）所称事项规定操作和程序，可以具体规定这些程序中某些或者全部操作和程序可以由出席程序的主管委员确定。

废止

40　［废止 2012-16-29.］

Part 5   Hearings and Appeals

Panels

41 (1) The benchers may make rules providing for any of the
following:

   (a) the appointment and composition of panels;

   (b) the practice and procedure for proceedings before
panels.

  (2) A panel may order an applicant or respondent, or a
shareholder, director, officer or employee of a respondent
law corporation, to do either or both of the following:

   (a) give evidence under oath or by affirmation;

   (b) at any time before or during a hearing, produce all
files and records that are in the possession of that
person and that may be relevant to a matter under
consideration.

Failure to attend

42 (1) This section applies if an applicant or respondent fails to
attend or remain in attendance at

第 5 节　听证和上诉

专责小组

41　（1）主管委员可以制定规则，规定任何下列事项：

（a）专责小组的任命和组成；

（b）专责小组处理的案件的操作和程序。

（2）专责小组可以命令申请人或者应诉人，或者被诉法律公司的股东、董事、职员或者雇员，从事下列活动之一或者二者：

（a）在宣誓或者郑重声明后作证；

（b）在听证之前或者过程中的任何时候，出示该人所持有的可能与正在审议的事项有关的全部卷宗和记录。

未能出席

42　（1）在申请人或者应诉人未能出席下列程序或者未能在下列程序中保持出席状态的情况下，本条适用：

(a) a hearing on an application for enrolment as an articled student, call and admission, or reinstatement,

(b) a hearing on a citation, or

(c) a review on the record by a review board under section 47.

(2) If satisfied that the applicant or respondent has been served with notice of the hearing or review, the panel or the review board may proceed with the hearing or review in the absence of the applicant or respondent and make any order that the panel or the review board could have made in the presence of the applicant or respondent.

Right to counsel

43   (1) An applicant, a respondent or a person who is the subject of a proceeding may appear at any hearing with counsel.

(2) The society may employ or retain legal or other assistance in conducting an investigation under Part 2, 3 or 4 or on the issue of a citation and may be represented by counsel at any hearing.

Witnesses

44   (1) In this section:

"**party**" means an applicant, a respondent or the society;

"**tribunal**" means the benchers, a review board or a panel, or a member of the benchers, a review board or a panel, as the context requires.

(2) For the purposes of a proceeding under Part 2, 3, 4 or 5 of

（a）关于作为见习生注册的申请、认许和准入或者恢复执业的听证，

（b）关于传唤证的听证，或者

（c）审查委员会根据第 47 条对记录的审查。

（2）如果确信已经向申请人或者应诉人送达了听证或者审查通知，在申请人或者应诉人缺席的情况下，专责小组或者审查委员会可以继续进行听证或者审查，作出专责小组或者审查委员会在申请人或者应诉人在场情况下本可以作出的命令。

获得律师帮助权

43　（1）申请人、应诉人或者作为程序的主题的人，可以与律师一同出席任何听证。

（2）在根据第 2 节、第 3 节或者第 4 节进行调查，或者在就传唤证问题进行调查时，律师协会可以雇用或者聘用法律或者其他帮助，可以在任何听证中由律师代理。

证人

44　（1）在本条中：

"当事人" 是指申请人、应诉人或者律师协会；

"裁判庭" 是指主管委员、审查委员会或者专责小组，或者主管委员、审查委员会或者专责小组的成员，视上下文而定。

（2）为根据本法第 2 节、第 3 节、第 4 节或者第 5 节进行的

this Act, a party may prepare and serve a summons, in a form established in the rules, requiring a person to attend an oral or electronic hearing to give evidence, on oath or affirmation or in any other manner, that is admissible and relevant to an issue in the proceeding.

(3) A party may apply to the Supreme Court for an order directing

(a) a person to comply with a summons served by a party under subsection (2),

(b) any directors and officers of a person to cause the person to comply with a summons served by a party under subsection (2), or

(c) the custodian of a penal institution or another person who has custody of a person who is the subject of the summons to ensure the person in custody attends the hearing.

(4) For the purposes of a proceeding under Part 2, 3, 4 or 5 of this Act, a tribunal may make an order requiring a person

(a) to attend an oral or electronic hearing to give evidence, on oath or affirmation or in any other manner, that is admissible and relevant to an issue in the proceeding, or

(b) to produce for the tribunal or a party a document or other thing in the person's possession or control, as specified by the tribunal, that is admissible and relevant to an issue in the proceeding.

(5) A tribunal may apply to the Supreme Court for an order directing

程序之目的，当事人可以制定并送达规则规定的形式的传票，要求某人出席口头或者电子听证，以宣誓、郑重陈述或者任何其他方式作证，提供在程序中可采的与争议点相关的证据。

（3）当事人可以向最高法院申请命令，指令：

（a）某人遵守当事人根据（2）送达的传票，

（b）某人的任何董事或者职员敦促该人遵守当事人根据（2）送达的传票，或者

（c）刑罚执行机关的看守人或者羁押作为传票对象的人员的他人，确保羁押中的该人出席听证。

（4）为根据本法第2节、第3节、第4节或者第5节进行的程序之目的，裁判庭可以作出命令要求某人：

（a）出席口头或者电子听证，经宣誓或者郑重声明或者采用任何其他方式作证，提供在程序中可采的与争议点相关的证据，或者

（b）向裁判庭或者当事人出示该人持有或者控制的裁判庭具体列明的可采并与程序中的争议点相关的文件或者其他物品。

（5）裁判庭可以向最高法院申请命令，指令：

(a) a person to comply with an order made by the tribunal under subsection (4),

(b) any directors and officers of a person to cause the person to comply with an order made by the tribunal under subsection (4), or

(c) the custodian of a penal institution or another person who has custody of a person who is the subject of an order made by the tribunal under subsection (4) to ensure the person in custody attends the hearing.

(6) On an application under subsection (3) or (5), the Supreme Court may make the order requested or another order it considers appropriate.

Application of Administrative Tribunals Act

44.1 (1) For the purposes of a proceeding under Part 2, 3, 4 or 5 of this Act, sections 48, 49 and 56 of the Administrative Tribunals Act apply, subject to the following:

(a) "decision maker" in section 56 means a member of the benchers, of a review board or of a panel;

(b) "tribunal" in those sections has the same meaning as in section 44 (1).

(2) A tribunal may apply to the Supreme Court for an order directing a person to comply with an order referred to in section 48 of the Administrative Tribunals Act, and the court may make the order requested or another order it considers appropriate.

（a）某人遵守裁判庭根据（4）作出的命令，

（b）该人的任何董事或者职员敦促该人遵守裁判庭根据（4）作出的命令，或者

（c）刑罚执行机关的看守人或者羁押作为裁判庭根据（4）作出的命令的对象的人员的他人，确保羁押中的该人出席听证。

（6）就根据（3）或者（5）提出的申请，最高法院可以作出所请求的命令，或者作出它认为适当的其他命令。

《行政裁判庭法》的适用

44.1　（1）在遵守下列规定的情况下，为根据本法第 2 节、第 3 节、第 4 节或者第 5 节进行的程序之目的，《行政裁判庭法》第 48 条、第 49 条和第 56 条适用：

（a）第 56 条的"决定作出者"是指主管委员、审查委员会或者专责小组的成员；

（b）这些条文中的"裁判庭"的含义见 44（1）。

（2）裁判庭可以向最高法院申请命令，指令某人遵守《行政裁判庭法》第 48 条所称命令，法院可以作出所请求的命令，或者作出它认为适当的其他命令。

Repealed

45 [Repealed 2012-16-34.]

Society request for evidence

45.1 (1) On application by the society, if it appears to the Supreme Court that a person outside British Columbia may have evidence that may be relevant to an investigation or a hearing under this Act, the Supreme Court may issue a letter of request directed to the judicial authority of the jurisdiction in which the person who may have evidence is believed to be located.

(2) A letter of request issued under subsection (1) must be

(a) signed by a judge of the Supreme Court, and

(b) provided to the society for use under subsection (5) .

(3) A letter of request issued under subsection (1) may request the judicial authority to which it is directed to do one or more of the following:

(a) order the person referred to in the letter of request to be examined under oath in the manner, at the place and by the date referred to in the letter of request;

(b) in the case of an examination for the purposes of a hearing, order that a person who is a party to the hearing is entitled to

(i) be present or represented by counsel during the examination, and

废止

45　[废止 2012-16-34.]

律师协会请求证据

45.1　（1）经律师协会申请，如果在最高法院看来，不列颠哥伦比亚之外的人可能有可能与根据本法进行的调查或者听证有关的证据，最高法院可以签发证据要求书致可能有证据的人员据信所在司法辖区的司法当局。

（2）根据（1）签发的证据要求书必须：

（a）由最高法院法官签名，并且

（b）根据（5）提供给律师协会使用。

（3）根据（1）签发的证据要求书可以请求其所致司法当局从事下列一个或者多个活动：

（a）证据要求书所称人员在证据要求书所称的地点和期日，宣誓后接受询问；

（b）在为听证目的进行询问的情况下，命令作为听证当事人的人员有权：

（i）在询问期间，出席或者由法律顾问代理，以及

(ii) examine the person referred to in paragraph (a);

(c) appoint a person as the examiner to conduct the examination;

(d) order the person to be examined to produce at the examination a record or thing specified in the letter of request;

(e) direct that the evidence obtained by the examination be recorded and certified in the manner specified in the letter of request;

(f) take any other action that the Supreme Court considers appropriate.

(4) The failure of a person entitled under subsection (3)

(b) to be present or represented by counsel during an examination or to examine the person referred to in subsection (3)(a) does not prevent the society from reading in the evidence from the examination at a hearing, if the examination has otherwise been conducted in accordance with the letter of request.

(5) The society must send a letter of request issued under subsection (1):

(a) if an examination is to be held in Canada, to the Deputy Attorney General for the Province of British Columbia, or

(b) if an examination is to be held outside Canada, to the Under Secretary of State for Foreign Affairs of Canada.

(6) A letter of request must have attached to it all of the

（ii）询问（a）所称人员；

（c）指定一个人作为询问者进行询问；

（d）命令被询问的人在询问时出示证据要求书具体列
　　明的记录或者物品；

（e）指令对通过询问获得的证据按照证据要求书具体规
　　定的方式进行记录和核证；

（f）采取最高法院认为适当的任何其他行动。

（4）（3）（b）规定的有权人员在询问时未能出席或者得到法
　　律顾问的代理，或者未能询问（3）（a）所称人员，在
　　已经遵照证据要求书进行了询问的情况下，并不禁止律
　　师协会在听证时将该询问读为证据。

（5）律师协会必须向下列人员发出根据（1）签发的证据要
　　求书：
　　（a）如果询问是在加拿大举行的，不列颠哥伦比亚省副
　　　　总检察长，或者

　　（b）如果询问是在加拿大外举行的，加拿大外交部副
　　　　部长。

（6）证据要求书必须附有所有下列事项：

following:

(a) any questions to be put to the person to be examined;

(b) if known, the name, address and telephone number of

    (i) the solicitor or agent of the society,

    (ii) the person to be examined, and

    (iii) if applicable, the person entitled under subsection (3)(b) to be present or represented by counsel during the examination and to examine the person referred to in subsection (3)(a);

(c) a translation of the letter of request and any questions into the official language of the jurisdiction where the examination is to take place, if necessary, along with a certificate of the translator, bearing the full name and address of the translator, and certifying that the translation is a true and complete translation.

(7) The society must file with the Deputy Attorney General for the Province of British Columbia or with the Under Secretary of State for Foreign Affairs of Canada, as the case may be, an undertaking to be responsible for any charge and expense incurred by either of them in relation to the letter of request and to pay them on receiving notification from them of the amount.

(8) This section does not limit any power the society may have to obtain evidence outside British Columbia by any other means.

(9) The making of an order by a judicial authority in accordance with a letter of request issued under subsection (1) does

（a）向被询问人员提出的任何问题；

（b）在知道的情况下，下列人员的姓名、地址和电话号码：

　　（i）律师协会的事务律师或者代理人，

　　（ii）被询问的人，以及

　　（iii）在适用的情况下，根据（3）（b）有权在询问时在场或者由法律顾问代理的人员和（3）（a）所称对该人进行询问的人员；

（c）在必要情况下，使用询问发生地司法辖区官方语言翻译的证据要求书和任何提问的译本，并附有载有译者的全名和地址的证明，并核证该译本是真实和完整的翻译。

（7）律师协会必须向不列颠哥伦比亚省副总检察长或者加拿大外交部副部长（视情况而定）提交承诺，说明对他们就证据要求书发生的任何手续费和耗费负责，并在他们收到关于款额的通知时支付该款额。

（8）本条并不限制律师协会就以任何其他方式在不列颠哥伦比亚之外取得证据所可能拥有的任何权力。

（9）司法当局遵照根据（1）签发的证据要求书作出命令时，并不确定根据该命令所获得的证据在听证中是否可采为证据。

not determine whether evidence obtained under the order is admissible in evidence in a hearing.

(10) Unless otherwise provided by this section, the practice and procedure for appointing a person, conducting an examination and certifying and returning the appointment under this section, as far as possible, is the same as the practice and procedure that govern similar matters in civil proceedings in the Supreme Court.

Costs

46 (1) The benchers may make rules governing the assessment of costs by a panel, a review board or a committee under this Act including:

(a) the time allowed for payment of costs, and

(b) the extension of time for payment of costs.

(2) If legal assistance employed by the benchers is provided by an employee of the society, the amount of costs that may be awarded under the rules in respect of that legal assistance may be the same as though the society had retained outside counsel.

(3) The amount of costs ordered to be paid by a respondent or applicant under the rules may be recovered as a debt owing to the society and, when collected, the amount is the property of the society.

(4) For the purpose of recovering a debt under subsection (3) , the executive director may

（10）除非本条另有规定，根据本条与某人预约、进行询问、确认预约的做法和程序，应当尽可能与最高法院民事程序中调整类似事项的做法和程序相同。

成本

46　（1）主管委员可以制定规则，调整专责小组、审查委员会或者委员会根据本法进行的成本评定，包括：

（a）允许支付成本的时间，以及

（b）延长支付成本的时间。

（2）如果主管委员使用的帮助是律师协会的雇员提供的，就像律师协会聘请的是外部法律顾问那样，就其法律帮助的成本，根据规则进行判赔。

（3）根据规则命令由应诉人或者申请人支付的成本，可以作为对律师协会的债务进行追讨，在追回后，该款额是律师协会的财产。

（4）为根据（3）追讨债务，执行主任可以：

(a) issue a certificate stating that the amount of costs is due, the amount remaining unpaid, including interest, and the name of the person required to pay it, and

(b) file the certificate with the Supreme Court.

(5) A certificate filed under subsection (4) with the Supreme Court is of the same effect, and proceedings may be taken on it, as if it were a judgment of the Supreme Court for the recovery of a debt in the amount stated against the person named in it.

Review on the record

47 (1) Within 30 days after being notified of the decision of a panel under section 22 (3) or 38 (5), (6) or (7), the applicant or respondent may apply in writing for a review on the record by a review board.

(2) Within 30 days after the decision of a panel under section 22 (3), the credentials committee may refer the matter for a review on the record by a review board.

(3) Within 30 days after the decision of a panel under section 38 (4), (5), (6) or (7), the discipline committee may refer the matter for a review on the record by a review board.

(3.1) Within 30 days after an order for costs assessed under a rule made under section 27 (2) (e) or 46, an applicant, a respondent or a lawyer who is the subject of the order may apply in writing for a review on the record by a review board.

（a）签发证明，说明所欠成本的数额、仍然未付的数额，
包括利息，以及需要支付这些款额的人员的姓名，
以及

（b）将该证明提交最高法院。

（5）根据（4）向最高法院存档的证明，与最高法院作出的向
其列名者追讨所载数额的债务的判决具有同等效力，可
以据此提起程序。

记录审查

47　（1）在就专责小组根据 22（3）或者 38（5）、（6）或者（7）
作出的决定得到通知后 30 日内，申请人或者应诉人可以
以书面形式申请由审查委员会对记录进行审查。

（2）在专责小组根据 22（3）作出决定后 30 日内，资质委员
会可以将事务移送审查委员会就记录进行审查。

（3）在专责小组根据 38（4）、（5）、（6）或者（7）作出决定
后 30 日内，惩戒委员会可以将事务移送审查委员会就记
录进行审查。

（3.1）在根据依 27（2）（e）或者 46 制定的规则作出成本评定
命令后 30 日内，作为命令的对象的申请人、应诉人或
者律师，可以以书面形式申请由审查委员会对记录进行
审查。

(3.2) Within 30 days after an order for costs assessed by a panel under a rule made under section 46, the credentials or discipline committee may refer the matter for a review on the record by a review board.

(4) If, in the opinion of a review board, there are special circumstances, the review board may hear evidence that is not part of the record.

(4.1) [Repealed 2012-16-36.]

(5) After a hearing under this section, the review board may

(a) confirm the decision of the panel, or

(b) substitute a decision the panel could have made under this Act.

(6) The benchers may make rules providing for one or more of the following:

(a) the appointment and composition of review boards;

(b) establishing procedures for an application for a review under this section;

(c) the practice and procedure for proceedings before review boards.

Appeal

48 (1) Subject to subsection (2) , any of the following persons who are affected by a decision, determination or order of a panel or of a review board may appeal the decision, determination or order to the Court of Appeal:

(a) an applicant;

（3.2）在专责小组根据依第 46 条作出成本评定命令后 30 日内，资质或者惩戒委员会可以将事务移送审查委员会就记录进行审查。

（4）如果在审查委员会看来，存在特殊情形，审查委员会可以听取并不构成记录之一部分的证据。

（4.1）[废止 2012-16-36.]

（5）在根据本条进行听证后，审查委员会可以：

（a）维持专责小组的决定，或者

（b）替代专责小组本可以根据本法作出的命令。

（6）主管委员可以制定规则，就下列一个或者多个事项作出规定：

（a）审查委员会的任命和组成；

（b）建立根据本条提出审查申请的程序；

（c）审查委员会处理的程序的操作和程序。

上诉

48（1）在遵守（2）的情况下，受到专责小组或者审查委员会的决议、决定或者命令影响的任何下列人员，可以就该决议、决定或者命令上诉于上诉法院：

（a）申请人；

(b) a respondent;

(c) a lawyer who is suspended or disbarred under this Act;

(d) the society.

(2) An appeal by the society under subsection (1) is limited to an appeal on a question of law.

　　（b）应诉人；

　　（c）根据本法被停止执业或者取消律师资格的律师；

　　（d）律师协会。

（2）律师协会根据（1）提出的上诉限于法律问题。

Part 6 Custodianships

Definitions

49   In this Part:

"court" means the Supreme Court;

"custodian" means a person appointed by an order under section 50 (2) or 54 (2) (b) ;

"practice" includes a law practice carried on by a lawyer on behalf of a law corporation whether as an employee of the law corporation or otherwise;

"property" includes books, records, accounts, funds, securities and any other real or personal property, wherever located:

(a) within a lawyer's possession or control, if held or used by the lawyer for the benefit of a client or other person, or otherwise held or used in the lawyer's capacity as a barrister and solicitor,

(b) in the possession or control of a person other than a lawyer if the lawyer has a duty to account to a client or other person for the property, or

(c) referred to in paragraph (a) or (b) , if held or used by a corporation, including a law corporation.

第 6 节　保管

定义

49　在本节中：

"法院"是指最高法院；

"保管人"是指根据 50（2）或者 54（2）（b）作出的命令所任命的人员；

"执业活动"包括律师代表法律公司开展的法律执业活动，无论是否作为法律公司的雇员或者其他人员；

"财产"包括下列账簿、记录、账户、资金、证券和任何其他动产和不动产，不论位于哪里：

（a）为律师持有或者控制，律师为委托人或者他人利益持有或者使用的，或者律师作为出庭律师和事务律师，以其他方式持有或者使用的账簿、记录、账户、资金、证券和任何其他动产和不动产，

（b）律师之外的人员持有或者控制的律师就此负有对委托人或者他人作出说明的职责的财产，或者

（c）公司（包括法律公司）持有或者使用的（a）或者（b）所称的账簿、记录、账户、资金、证券和任何其他动产和不动产。

Appointment of custodian

50 (1) The society may apply to the court, with or without notice to anyone, for an order appointing a practising lawyer or the society as a custodian of the practice of another lawyer to

(a) take possession of or control over all or part of the property of the lawyer, and

(b) determine the status of, manage, arrange for the conduct of and, if appropriate, terminate the practice of the lawyer.

(2) The court may grant a custodianship order applied for under subsection (1) if, in the opinion of the court, sufficient grounds exist.

(3) Without limiting the discretion of the court to grant an order under subsection (2) , sufficient grounds for the appointment of a custodian of a lawyer's practice exist if the lawyer

(a) consents to the appointment of a custodian,

(b) dies, resigns or otherwise terminates membership in the society,

(c) is unable to practise as a lawyer because of physical or mental illness or for any other reason,

(d) disappears or neglects or abandons the practice of law, or

(e) is disbarred or suspended from the practice of law in British Columbia or any other jurisdiction.

(4) When a law corporation carries on the business of providing legal services to the public through a lawyer who is the

指定保管人

50 （1）律师协会可以向法院申请命令，无论是否通知他人，以
　　　任命执业律师或者律师协会作为其他律师的执业活动的
　　　保管人：

　　　（a）持有或者控制该律师的全部或者部分财产，以及

　　　（b）确定律师的业务的状态，管理、安排进行律师的业
　　　　　务，以及在适当情况下终止律师的业务。

　　（2）如果在法院看来，存在充分根据，法院可以作出根据（1）
　　　申请的保管人命令。

　　（3）在不限制法院根据（2）作出命令的自由裁量权的情况下，
　　　如果律师存在下列情况，则存在就律师的业务任命保管
　　　人的充分根据：

　　　（a）同意指定保管人，
　　　（b）死亡、退会或者以其他方式终止了在律师协会的会
　　　　　员资格，
　　　（c）因生理或者精神疾病，或者因为任何其他原因，不
　　　　　能够作为律师执业，
　　　（d）失踪或者疏怠、抛弃法律执业活动，或者
　　　（e）在不列颠哥伦比亚或者任何其他司法辖区被取消律
　　　　　师资格或者被停止从事法律执业活动。
　　（4）当法律公司通过其是本条规定的申请的对象的律师开展
　　　向公众提供法律服务的业务时，法院可以命令根据（2）

subject of an application under this section, the court may order the custodian appointed under subsection (2) to

(a) take possession of or control over all or part of the law corporation's property, and

(b) determine the status of, manage, arrange for the conduct of and, if appropriate, terminate the practice of the law corporation.

(5) An order under this section must direct that any person receiving notice of the order must retain all the lawyer's property that is within or comes into that person's possession or control, until directed otherwise by the custodian or by an order of the court.

(6) An order under this section may

(a) direct the sheriff to search for, seize, remove and place into the possession or control of the custodian all or part of the lawyer's property,

(b) authorize the sheriff, for the purpose of paragraph (a), to enter

(i) any building or place other than the lawyer's dwelling house and open any safety deposit box or other receptacle, and

(ii) the lawyer's dwelling house and open any safe or other receptacle, if there are grounds to believe that the lawyer's property may be found there,

(c) direct any savings institution or other person to deal with, hold or dispose of the lawyer's property as the court directs, and to deliver to the custodian or

指定的保管人：

（a）持有或者控制法律公司的全部或者部分财产，以及

（b）确定法律公司的业务的状态，管理、安排进行法律
　　　公司的执业活动，以及在适当情况下终止法律公司
　　　的执业活动。

（5）根据本条作出的命令必须指令所有收到命令通知的人员
　　　必须保有处于或者受到该人持有或者控制的所有律师的
　　　财产，直至保管人或者法院命令作出指示。

（6）根据本条作出的命令可以：

（a）指令治安官搜查、扣押、移动律师的全部或者部分
　　　财产并置于保管人持有或者控制之下，

（b）授权治安官为（a）之目的，进入：

（i）律师住宅之外的任何建筑物或者场所并打开任
　　　何保险箱或者其他容器；

（ii）律师的住宅并打开任何保险箱或者其他容器，如
　　　果有根据认为可以在那里找到律师的财产的话，

（c）就下列一项或者多项内容，指令任何储蓄机构或者
　　　其他人员按照法院指令，处理、持有或者处置律师
　　　的财产，以及按照法院指令，提交保管人或者采取

otherwise, as the court directs, one or more of the following:

(i) the lawyer's property;

(ii) a copy of records relating to the lawyer's practice;

(iii) a copy of other records, when it is necessary for the effective conduct of the custodianship to do so,

(d) give directions to the custodian respecting the disposition of the lawyer's property and the manner in which the custodianship should be conducted,

(e) give directions as to the service of an order made or notice required under this Part,

(f) include other orders or give other directions to facilitate the conduct of the custodianship, and

(g) if the lawyer is a person referred to in section 15 (3) (a) or (b), prohibit the lawyer from acting as any or all of the following until the lawyer is a member in good standing of the society or until the court orders otherwise:

(i) a personal representative of a deceased person;

(ii) a trustee of the estate of a deceased person;

(iii) a committee under the Patients Property Act;

(iii.1) an attorney under Part 2 of the Power of Attorney Act;

(iv) a representative under the Representation Agreement Act.

(7) Unless otherwise directed by the court, the custodian must cause an order made under this Part to be served promptly

其他行动:

（ⅰ）律师的财产;

（ⅱ）与律师的执业活动有关的记录的复制件;

（ⅲ）进行有效保管所必需的其他记录的复制件,

（d）就保管人就律师的财产处置以及进行保管的方式对
保管人作出指令,

（e）就送达根据本节作出的命令或者所要求的通知作出
指令,

（f）包括其他命令或者作出其他指令,以促进保管,以及

（g）如果律师是 15（3）（a）或者（b）所称人员,禁止
律师担任下列任何或者全部职务,直至律师成为
律师协会资格完好的会员,或者直至法院作出其
他命令:

（ⅰ）已故人员的个人代表;

（ⅱ）已故人员的遗产的受托人;

（ⅲ）《患者财产法》规定的委员会;

（ⅲ.1）《授权委托法》第 2 节规定的律师;

（ⅳ）《代理协议法》规定的代理人。

（7）除非法院另有指令,保管人必须敦促迅速向律师送达根
据本节作出的命令。

on the lawyer.

(8) A sheriff, deputy sheriff or court bailiff executing an order under this Part has the same powers as that person has in the execution of a writ of seizure and sale.

If society appointed as custodian

50.1 If the society is appointed as a custodian, the executive director must

(a) designate a person who is

(i) an employee of the society, and

(ii) a practising lawyer, or

(b) retain the services of a practising lawyer

to perform the duties and functions and exercise the powers of a custodian on behalf of the society.

Powers of custodian

51 A custodian may do any or all of the following:

(a) notify a client of the lawyer, or any other person, of the custodian's appointment, and may communicate with that client or person respecting the conduct of the custodianship;

(b) represent a client of the lawyer, in place of that lawyer, in any cause or matter in respect of which that lawyer was acting at the time a custodian was appointed, to the extent necessary to preserve the interests of the client;

(c) conduct or authorize an investigation of the property of the lawyer;

（8）执行根据本节作出的命令的治安官，副治安官或者法警，
　　拥有在执行扣押和变卖财产令时一样的权力。

如果律师协会被指定为保管人

50.1　如果律师协会被指定为保管人，执行主任必须：

　　（a）指派下列人员：

　　　　（i）律师协会的雇员，并且

　　　　（ii）执业律师，或者

　　（b）聘请执业律师的服务

来代表律师协会履行保管人的职责和功能，并行使其权力。

保管人的权力

51　保管人可以从事下列任何或者全部活动：

　　（a）就保管人的指定，通知律师的委托人或者任何其他人员，
　　　　并且可以同该委托人或者人员进行交流；

　　（b）在保护委托人利益合理必需的范围内，在保管人被指定
　　　　时律师正在办理的任何事由或者事项中，取代律师来代
　　　　理律师的委托人；

　　（c）调查或者授权调查律师的财产；

(d) require from the lawyer or any other person records and information that may be reasonably necessary to facilitate the conduct of the custodianship and, if necessary, apply to the court for an order to enforce the requirement;

(e) report to an insurer any facts of which the custodian becomes aware that indicate that the lawyer in that lawyer's professional capacity may be liable to a client or other person;

(f) cooperate with an insurer respecting any claim arising out of the lawyer's practice, to the extent required by the policy;

(g) advise a client or other person of any facts of which the custodian becomes aware that may give rise to a claim for payment under section 31;

(h) deal with the assets and liabilities of the lawyer's practice to the extent necessary to protect the interests of clients and, subject to the interests of clients,

  (i) pay all or part of the expenses and disbursements of and incidental to any acts done or proceedings taken under this Part, and

  (ii) preserve the value of the practice;

(i) employ or retain assistance in the conduct of the custodianship.

Society access to property

52 (1) The executive director may at any time examine and make copies of any of the lawyer's property in the possession or control of the custodian.

（d）向律师或者任何其他人员要求促进保管可能合理必需的记录和信息，在必要时，向法院申请命令来执行该要求；

（e）向保险商报告保管人意识到的表明律师以其律师职业身份可能要对委托人或者他人承担责任的任何事实；

（f）就律师的执业活动所引发的任何索赔，在保单要求的范围内与保险商合作；

（g）向委托人或者他人告知保管人意识到的可能导致第 31 条规定的付款主张的任何事实；

（h）在保护委托人的利益所必需的范围内，处理律师的执业活动的财产和责任，并且在保护委托人利益的情况下：

（i）支付根据本节采取的任何行动或者程序所发生的或者附带发生的全部或者部分耗费和支出，以及

（ii）保存业务的价值；

（i）在保管时雇用或者聘请帮助。

律师协会近用财产

52 （1）执行主任可以在任何时候检查并且复制保管人持有或者控制的律师的任何财产。

(2) Copies made under subsection (1) must be made at the society's expense and only for its own use.

Property in the custody of a custodian

53 (1) A custodian may deliver property in the custodian's possession or control to a person claiming it if the custodian is satisfied that

(a) the person is entitled to the property,

(b) no solicitor's lien exists or appears to exist in relation to it, and

(c) the executive director has been given a reasonable opportunity to examine the property under section 52.

(2) A lawyer whose property is in the custody of a custodian under this Part may make a claim for a solicitor's lien in relation to any part of the property by filing notice of a claim for lien with the custodian.

(3) A notice under subsection (2) must

(a) be in writing,

(b) be filed within 30 days after service on the lawyer of the order under section 50 (2), and

(c) give full particulars of the claim.

(4) On receiving a notice under subsection (2), the custodian must promptly give written notice of the claim for lien to the apparent owner of the property on which the lien is claimed, and the rights of the parties must then be determined according to law.

（2）根据（1）制作复制件，其费用必须由律师协会来支付，且仅为它自己使用。

保管人保管的财产

53 （1）在保管人确信下列情况下，保管人可以将其持有或者控制的财产移交主张这些财产的人员：

（a）该人有权取得该财产，

（b）就该财产不存在或者看起来不存在事务律师的留置权，以及

（c）执行主任有合理机会根据第 52 条检查该财产。

（2）根据本节其财产处于保管人保管下的律师，可以通过向保管人提交留置权主张通知，就该财产的任何部分主张事务律师的留置权。

（3）根据（2）进行的通知必须：
（a）采用书面形式，
（b）在 50（2）规定的命令送达律师后 30 日内提交，以及

（c）对该主张进行详细说明。
（4）在收到（2）规定的通知后，保管人必须迅速将该留置权主张的书面通知送达被主张留置权的财产的明显所有人，然后必须依法确定当事人的权利。

(5) If a lawyer fails to file a claim of lien under this section within the period referred to in subsection (3) , the custodian may deliver the property to the person entitled to it if the custodian is otherwise satisfied that it is proper to do so.

Applications to the court

54 (1) A custodian, the society, the lawyer concerned or any other interested person may apply to the court for an order under this section, with or without notice to anyone.

(2) On an application under subsection (1) , the court may do one or more of the following:

(a) discharge the custodian, unless the society shows cause why the custodianship should be continued;

(b) appoint another practising lawyer or the society as a custodian;

(c) make any other order provided for in section 50 (4) , in which case section 50 (5) and (6) applies;

(d) summarily determine the validity of a claim to a solicitor's lien;

(e) make no order.

(3) Despite anything in this Part, the court may at any time extend or shorten the time within which anything is required to be done or dispense with any of the requirements of this Part.

（5）在律师未能在（3）所称期间内根据本条提出留置要求的
情况下，保管人可以将该财产移交有权取得它的人员，
如果保管人确信这么做适当的话。

向法院提出申请

54 （1）保管人、律师协会、有关律师或者任何其他利害关系人，
可以根据本条向法院申请命令，无论有无对任何人进行
通知。

（2）就根据（1）提出的申请，法院可以从事下列一个或者多
个活动：

（a）解除保管，除非律师协会申明了为什么保管应当继
续存在的理由；

（b）指定其他执业律师或者律师协会担任保管人；

（c）在 50（5）和（6）适用的情况下，作出 50（4）规定
的任何其他命令；

（d）速决确定关于事务律师留置权的主张的有效性；

（e）不作出命令。

（3）尽管有本节的任何规定，法院可以在任何时候延长或者
缩短需要去做的事情的时间，或者免除本节的任何要求。

Custodianship rules

55   The benchers may make rules regarding custodianships, including rules imposing duties on a lawyer whose practice is the subject of a custodianship authorized under this Part.

Liability and costs

56   (1) Section 86 applies to protect a custodian, the society and a person acting for either of them, for anything done or not done by one of them in good faith while acting or purporting to act under this Part.

(2) No costs may be awarded against a custodian, the society or a person acting for either of them, for anything done or not done by any of them in good faith while acting or purporting to act under this Part.

(3) Unless the court otherwise orders, the lawyer or the estate of a deceased lawyer must pay to the society the fees, expenses and disbursements of and incidental to any acts done or proceedings taken under this Part, including the fees, expenses and disbursements of a custodian.

(4) Part 8 applies to payment for fees, expenses and disbursements under subsection (3) of this section.

保管规则

55　主管委员可以就保管制定规则，包括就其执业活动是本节授权的保管的对象的律师设定职责的规则。

责任和成本

56　（1）第 86 条适用于保护保管人、律师协会或者为二者行为的人员就其善意根据本节或者宣称根据本节所做的或者没有做的任何行为。

（2）就保管人、律师协会或者为二者行为的人员就其善意根据本节或者宣称根据本节所做的或者没有做的任何行为，不得判赔任何成本。

（3）除非法院另有命令，律师或者已故律师的遗产必须向律师协会支付根据本节采取的行为或者程序所发生的或者附带发生的费用、耗费和支出，包括保管人的费用、耗费和支出。

（4）第 8 节适用于根据本条（3）支付的律师费、耗费和支出。

Part 7   Law Foundation

Definitions

57   In this Part:

"board" means the board of governors of the foundation;

"governor" means a member of the board.

Law Foundation of British Columbia

58   (1) The Law Foundation is continued as a corporation with the name "Law Foundation of British Columbia" consisting of the members of the board appointed under section 59 (1).

(2) The foundation may acquire, dispose of and otherwise deal with its property for the purposes of the foundation.

Board of governors

59   (1) The foundation is administered by a board of governors consisting of 18 governors as follows:

(a) the Attorney General or his or her appointee;

(b) 3 persons, not lawyers, appointed to the board by the

第 7 节   法律基金会

定义

57   在本节中：

"理事会" 是指基金会理事会；

"理事" 是指理事会成员。

不列颠哥伦比亚法律基金会

58 （1）法律基金会作为一个公司继续存在，其名称为"不列颠哥伦比亚法律基金会"，包括根据 59（1）任命的理事会成员。

　　（2）基金会可以为基金会目的取得、处置或者以其他方式处理其财产。

理事

59 （1）基金会由下列 18 名理事组成的理事会管理：

　　　（a）检察长或者其任命的人；

　　　（b）检察长任命到理事会的不是律师的 3 名人员；

Attorney General;

(c) 12 lawyers or judges appointed by the executive committee, of whom at least one must be from each county referred to in the County Boundary Act;

(d) 2 lawyers appointed by the executive committee of the British Columbia Branch of the Canadian Bar Association.

(2) Governors, other than the Attorney General, hold office for a term of 3 years or until their successors are appointed, and they may be re-appointed.

(3) The Attorney General may revoke the appointment of a governor appointed by the Attorney General, during that governor's term of office.

(4) The benchers may revoke the appointment of a governor appointed by the executive committee, during that governor's term of office.

(5) The Provincial Council of the British Columbia Branch of the Canadian Bar Association may revoke the appointment of a governor appointed by the executive committee of the branch, during that governor's term of office.

(6) The board must elect one governor to be chair of the board.

(7) If a vacancy occurs in the office of a governor, the person or body by whom the governor was appointed may appoint to the vacant office a person eligible to be appointed to that office by that person or body under subsection (1), and the person so appointed holds office for the balance of the term for which the governor was appointed, or until a

（c）执行委员会任命的 12 名律师或者法官，其中《县边
　　界法》所称的每个县至少有 1 名；

（d）加拿大律师协会不列颠哥伦比亚分支机构执行委员
　　会任命的 2 名律师。

（2）除了检察长外，理事的任期为 3 年，或者直至其继任者
　　被任命，他们可以获得再次任命。

（3）在理事任期内，检察长可以撤销其对理事的任命。

（4）在理事任期内，主管委员可以撤销执行委员会对理事的
　　任命。

（5）在理事任期内，加拿大律师协会不列颠哥伦比亚分支机构
　　省委员会可以撤销该分支机构执行委员会对理事的任命。

（6）理事会必须选举一名理事担任理事会主席。

（7）在理事职务缺位的情况下，任命理事的人员或者组织可
　　以将根据（1）有资格被该人员或者组织任命到该职务的
　　人员任命到空缺职务，该被任命的人员在该理事剩余任
　　期内任职，或者直至继任者被任命。

successor is appointed.

(8) The continuing governors may act despite a vacancy in the board.

(9) An act of the board is not invalid because of a defect that is afterwards discovered in the appointment of one or more governors.

(10) An appointed governor may resign from office on giving one month's notice in writing to the board of an intention to do so, and the resignation takes effect on the expiration of the notice or on its earlier acceptance by the board.

(11) A governor ceases to hold office if the governor

(a) ceases to hold the qualifications necessary for appointment,

(b) becomes a mentally disordered person,

(c) becomes bankrupt, or

(d) contravenes a provision of this Act or the rules, and a majority of the other governors considers that the contravention is sufficiently serious to justify the governor's removal from the board.

(12) A quorum of the board is 8 governors.

Bylaws

60   The board may make bylaws for purposes relating to the affairs, business, property and objects of the foundation including bylaws respecting the

(a) number and designation of officers of the foundation,

(b) appointment and terms of office of officers of the foundation

（8）尽管理事会存在缺位，存续的理事仍可以行动。

（9）理事会的行动并不因为事后发现其中一个或者多个理事的任命存在瑕疵而无效。

（10）经在 1 个月前就其意图向理事会发出书面通知，被任命的理事可以辞职，该辞职在通知届满时生效或者在其更早被理事会接受时生效。

（11）在理事出现下列情形的情况下，理事不再任职：

（a）不再具有任命所必需的资格，

（b）成为精神错乱的人，

（c）变得破产，或者

（d）违反了本法或者规则之规定，且大多数其他理事认为该违反行为的严重性足以支持免去其理事会职务。

（12）理事会的法定人数是 8 名理事。

章程

60　理事会可以为与事务、业务、财产和目标相关的目的制定章程，包括关于下列事项的章程：

（a）基金会职员的数量和选派，

（b）基金会职员的任命和任期，以及与其职务相关的所有事项，

and all matters relating to their offices,

(c) establishment of an executive committee and the delegation of powers to it,

(d) resignation or removal from office of officers of the foundation,

(e) number, designations and conditions of employment of employees of the foundation, other than officers,

(f) remuneration, if any, of officers of the foundation, and

(g) operation of the foundation's account.

Application of fund

61　(1) The purpose of the foundation is to establish and maintain a fund to be used for the following purposes:

(a) legal education;

(b) legal research;

(c) legal aid;

(d) law reform;

(e) establishing, operating and maintaining law libraries in British Columbia.

(2) The board may apply the funds of the foundation for the purposes of the foundation in the manner that the board may decide and may grant loans of the funds on terms and conditions the board determines.

(3) The foundation may employ or retain lawyers to advance the purposes of the foundation.

(4) The funds of the foundation consist of the following:

（c）建立执行委员会并将权力委派给它，

（d）基金会职员的辞职或者免职，

（e）基金会职员之外的雇员的数量、选派和雇用条件，

（f）基金会职员的薪酬（如果有的话），以及

（g）基金会账户的运营。

基金使用

61　（1）基金会的目的是为下列目的建立和保持基金：

（a）法律教育；

（b）法律研究；

（c）法律援助；

（d）法律改革；

（e）在不列颠哥伦比亚建立、运营和维护法律图书馆。

（2）主管委员会可以以理事会可以决定的方式为基金会目的使用基金会基金，可以用理事会确定的条件发放贷款。

（3）基金会可以雇用或者聘请律师来促进基金会的目的。

（4）基金会的基金包括：

(a) all money remitted to the foundation by or on behalf of lawyers under section 62 (2) or held in trust under section 63 (12) ;

(b) interest accruing from investment of the funds of the foundation;

(c) other money received by the foundation.

(5) The board may pay out of the funds of the foundation the costs, charges and expenses

(a) involved in the administration of the foundation, and

(b) incurred by the board in carrying out the purposes of the foundation.

(6) All money of the foundation must be paid into a savings institution designated under section 33 (3) (b) until invested or applied in accordance with this section, and that money must be used for the purposes of the foundation.

(7) Money that is not immediately required for the purposes of the foundation may be invested in the name of the foundation by the board in any manner in which trustees are authorized to invest trust funds.

(8) The accounts of the foundation must be audited annually by a chartered professional accountant appointed for that purpose by the board.

Interest on trust accounts

62 (1) A lawyer must deposit money received or held in trust in an interest bearing trust account at a savings institution

（a）由或者代表律师根据 62（2）汇给基金会的所有资金，
　　　或者根据 63（12）信托持有的资金；

（b）用基金会基金进行投资所收利息；

（c）基金会收到的其他资金。

（5）主管委员会可以用基金会基金支付下列活动中发生的成
　　本、手续费和耗费：

（a）管理基金会，以及

（b）理事会为基金会目的开展的活动。

（6）基金会所有资金必须付入根据 33（3）（b）指定的储蓄机
　　构，直至遵照本条投资或者使用，并且该资金必须用于
　　基金会目的。

（7）并不需要为基金会目的立即使用的资金，可以由理事会
　　以基金会名义以受托人受权投资信托基金的任何方式进
　　行投资。

（8）基金会的账户必须由理事会为审计目的指派的特许职业
　　会计师进行年度审计。

信托账户的利息

62　（1）律师收到或者信托持有的资金必须储蓄到根据 33（3）（b）
　　　　指定的储蓄机构的有息信托账户。

designated under section 33 (3) (b) .

(2) Subject to subsection (5) , a lawyer who is credited by a savings institution with interest on money received or held in trust,

(a) holds the interest in trust for the foundation, and

(b) must remit the interest to the foundation in accordance with the rules.

(3) The benchers may make rules

(a) permitting a lawyer to hold money in trust for more than one beneficiary in the same trust account, and

(b) respecting payment to the foundation of interest on trust accounts.

(4) A relationship between a lawyer and client or a trust relationship between a lawyer, as trustee, and the beneficiary of the trust does not make the lawyer liable to account to the client or beneficiary for interest received by the lawyer on money received or held in an account established under subsection (1) .

(5) On instruction from his or her client, a lawyer may place money held on behalf of the client in a separate trust account, in which case

(a) this section and the rules made under it do not apply, and

(b) interest paid on money in the account is the property of the client.

（2）在遵守（5）的情况下，就其收到或者信托持有的资金收
　　 到储蓄机构利息的律师：

　　 （a）为基金会信托持有利息，并且
　　 （b）必须遵照规则将利息汇给基金会。

（3）主管委员可以就下列事项制定规则：
　　 （a）允许律师为多个受益人在同一信托账户中持有信托
　　 　　 资金，以及
　　 （b）将信托账户中的利息支付给基金会。

（4）律师与委托人之间的关系或者律师作为受托人与信托受
　　 益人之间的信托关系，并不使得律师就在根据（1）设立
　　 的账户中收到或者持有的资金所收到的利息，有责任向
　　 委托人或者受益人作出说明。

（5）根据其委托人的指示，律师可以将代表委托人持有的资
　　 金存入单独的信托账户中，在这种情况下：

　　 （a）本条和根据本条制定的规则并不适用，以及

　　 （b）就账户中的资金支付的利息是委托人的财产。

Security and investment of trust funds

63　(1) In this section:

"**pooled trust funds**" means money that has been received by a lawyer in trust and that is not the subject of instructions under section 62 (5) ;

"**society trust account**" means a Law Society Pooled Trust Account established under subsection (5) .

(2) The benchers may make rules requiring that a lawyer do any or all of the following:

(a) use an approved form of agreement respecting the terms and conditions under which pooled trust funds will be held at designated savings institutions;

(b) tender the agreement, prepared and approved under paragraph (a) , at a designated savings institution before the lawyer deposits pooled trust funds at that savings institution;

(c) report annually to any savings institution into which the lawyer has deposited pooled trust funds the information required under the Canada Deposit Insurance Corporation Act.

(3) The society may enter into an agreement with a savings institution with whom lawyers have deposited pooled trust funds, respecting the investment and security of pooled trust funds on deposit at all branches of that savings institution.

(4) Without limiting subsection (3) , an agreement under that subsection may provide that

(a) pooled trust funds be transferred to the society, in

信托基金的安全和投资

63 （1）在本条中：

"集合信托基金" 是指律师因信托收到的，不是根据 62（5）作出的指示的对象的资金；

"律师协会信托账户" 是指根据（5）建立的律师协会集合信托账户。

  （2）主管委员可以制定规则，要求律师从事下列任何或者全部活动：

    （a）就指定的储蓄机构持有集合信托基金的条件，使用经过批准的协议格式；

    （b）律师在指定的储蓄机构储蓄集合信托基金之前，提供根据（a）拟定和批准的协议；

    （c）就加拿大《储蓄保险公司法》所要求的信息，向律师储蓄集合信托基金的任何储蓄机构进行年度报告。

  （3）律师协会可以与律师储蓄集合信托基金的储蓄机构，就在该储蓄机构所有分支机构储蓄的集合信托基金的投资和安全达成协议。

  （4）在不限制（3）的情况下，根据该款达成的协议可以规定：

    （a）集合信托基金转入律师协会，由其在（5）所称账户

trust, to be held in the account referred to in subsection (5) and to be invested in the manner permitted by subsection (6) , and

(b) the society obtain a line of credit, either secured or unsecured, from the savings institution for the purpose of ensuring that there is always sufficient money on deposit to guarantee that lawyers' trust cheques on their pooled trust fund accounts will be honoured.

(5) The society may establish and operate an account, to be known as a Law Society Pooled Trust Account, at any branch of the savings institution into which pooled trust funds may be deposited in accordance with an agreement under subsection (3) .

(6) Money in a society trust account may be invested in

(a) securities of Canada or a province,

(b) securities, the payment of the principal and interest of which is guaranteed by Canada or a province, or

(c) guaranteed trust or investment certificates of the savings institution that has the pooled trust account.

(7) Money earned on investments under subsection (6) may be used to

(a) purchase insurance in an amount that the society considers necessary to ensure that all lawyers' trust cheques drawn on their pooled trust fund accounts will be honoured, and

(b) pay service and other similar charges in respect of services provided by the savings institution at which the

中信托持有，并以（6）所允许的方式进行投资，
以及

（b）律师协会从储蓄机构获得信用额度（无论有无担保），
以确保总是有充足的资金存于储蓄机构，以保证律
师从集合信托基金账户开具的信托支票将得到承兑。

（5）律师协会可以遵照根据（3）达成的协议在可以储蓄集合
信托基金的储蓄机构的任何分支机构，建立和运营叫作
律师协会集合信托账户的账户。

（6）律师协会信托账户中的资金，可以投资于：

（a）加拿大或者某省的证券，

（b）本金和利息的支付由加拿大或者某个省担保的证券，
或者

（c）有着集合信托账户的储蓄机构担保的信托或者投资
证书。

（7）根据（6）进行投资所取得的资金，可以用于：

（a）购买律师协会认为确保所有律师从其集合信托基金
账户开具的信托支票将得到承兑所必需的保险额，
以及

（b）就律师协会根据（5）运营账户的储蓄机构提供的服
务，支付服务费和其他类似手续费。

society operates an account under subsection (5) .

(8) The society may pay money out of a society trust account to a person who has suffered a loss directly resulting from the inability or refusal of the savings institution to honour a lawyer's trust cheque drawn on a pooled trust fund account, up to a maximum, in any year, set by the benchers.

(9) The benchers must not pay out any money under subsection (8) unless they are satisfied that they will be reimbursed or indemnified, through agreements referred to in subsection (10) or the insurance purchased under subsection (7) , for any money that has been paid out.

(10) The society may enter into agreements with the Canada Deposit Insurance Corporation and the Credit Union Deposit Insurance Corporation of British Columbia respecting reimbursement or indemnity by those corporations of money that has been paid out under subsection (8) .

(11) The society may retain or employ a person to manage society trust accounts and may pay that person fees or remuneration out of interest earned on money in society trust accounts.

(12) Subject to subsections (7) , (8) and (11) , all interest earned on money deposited into a society trust account is held in trust by the society for the benefit of the foundation, and the society is not liable to account to any client of any lawyer in respect of that interest.

(13) Despite any agreement between a lawyer and a savings

（8）律师协会可以在任何年度用律师协会信托账户的资金，在主管委员确定的最高额度内，赔偿因储蓄机构不能或者拒绝承兑律师从集合信托基金账户开具的信托支票所遭受的直接损失的人员。

（9）主管委员不得根据（8）支付任何资金，除非他们确信他们将通过（10）所称协议或者根据（7）购买的保险，就支付的任何资金能得到偿还或者赔偿。

（10）律师协会可以与加拿大储蓄保险公司和不列颠哥伦比亚信用社储蓄保险公司就这些公司偿还或者赔偿根据（8）付出的资金达成协议。

（11）律师协会可以聘请或者雇用人员管理律师协会信托账户，并且可以用律师协会信托账户中所得利息向该人支付费用或者薪酬。

（12）在遵守（7）、（8）和（11）的情况下，就律师协会为基金会利益在律师协会信托账户中信托持有的储蓄资金所生全部利息，律师协会没有责任就该利息向任何律师的任何委托人作出说明。

（13）不论律师与储蓄机构达成何种协议，如果律师的集合信

institution, if the lawyer's pooled trust fund account is overdrawn by an amount exceeding $1 000, the savings institution must, as soon as practicable, inform the society of the particulars.

(14) Subsection (13) and the failure of a savings institution to comply with it has no effect on the civil liability of that savings institution to any person, and that liability, if any, must be determined as though that subsection were not in force.

托基金账户透支额超过 1 000 加元，储蓄机构必须尽可能早地将详情告知律师协会。

（14）（13）和储蓄机构未能遵守该规定，并不影响储蓄机构对任何人员的民事责任，如果存在该责任，必须像该款规定无效那样确定该责任。

Part 8   Lawyers' Fees

Definitions and interpretation

64   (1) In this Part:

"**agreement**" means a written contract respecting the fees, charges and disbursements to be paid to a lawyer or law firm for services provided or to be provided and includes a contingent fee agreement;

"**bill**" means a lawyer's written statement of fees, charges and disbursements;

"**charges**" includes taxes on fees and disbursements and interest on fees and disbursements;

"**contingent fee agreement**" means an agreement that provides that payment to the lawyer or law firm for services provided depends, at least in part, on the happening of an event;

"**court**" means the Supreme Court;

"**person charged**" includes a person who has agreed to pay for legal services, whether or not the services were provided on the person's behalf;

"**registrar**" means the registrar of the court.

(2) Unless otherwise ordered by the court, this Part, except sections 65, 66 (1) , 68, 77, 78 and 79 (1) , (2) , (3) , (6) and (7) , does not apply to a class proceeding within

第 8 节 律师费

定义和解释

64（1）在本节：

"**协议**"是指关于就提供的服务或者将要提供的服务支付给律师或者律师事务所的律师费、手续费和支出的书面合同，包括风险代理费协议；

"**账单**"是指律师关于律师费、手续费和支出的书面说明；

"**手续费**"包括律师费的税费和支出、律师费和支出的利息；

"**风险代理费协议**"是指规定因服务支付给律师或者律师事务所的款项取决于——至少在一定程度上取决于——某事件的发生的协议；

"**法院**"是指最高法院；

"**被收费人**"包括同意支付法律服务费用的人，无论该服务是否是为该人提供的；

"**司法常务官**"是指法院的司法常务官。

     （2）除非法院另有命令，本节除第 65 条、66（1）、第 68 条、第 77 条、第 78 条和 79（1）、（2）、（3）、（6）和（7）外，并不适用于《集团程序法》意义上的集团程序。

the meaning of the Class Proceedings Act.

(3) This Part applies to a lawyer's bill or agreement even though the lawyer has ceased to be a member of the society, if the lawyer was a member when the legal services were provided.

Agreement for legal services

65 (1) A lawyer or law firm may enter into an agreement with any other person, requiring payment for services provided or to be provided by the lawyer or law firm.

(2) Subsection (1) applies despite any law or usage to the contrary.

(3) A provision in an agreement that the lawyer is not liable for negligence, or that the lawyer is relieved from responsibility to which the lawyer would otherwise be subject as a lawyer, is void.

(4) An agreement under this section may be signed on behalf of a lawyer or law firm by an authorized agent who is a practising lawyer.

Contingent fee agreement

66 (1) Section 65 applies to contingent fee agreements.

(2) The benchers may make rules respecting contingent fee agreements, including, but not limited to, rules that do any of the following:

(a) limit the amount that lawyers or law firms may charge

（3）本节适用于律师的账单或者协议，即使律师已经不再是
　　律师协会会员，如果律师在提供法律服务时是律师协会
　　会员的话。

法律服务协议

65　（1）律师或者律师事务所可以与任何他人达成协议，要求就
　　　律师或者律师事务所提供或者将要提供的服务付费。

（2）尽管有任何相反的法律或者惯例，（1）也适用。

（3）协议中关于律师对过失不承担责任或者免除律师作为律
　　师本要承担的责任的规定无效。

（4）本条规定的协议可以由执业律师作为受权代理人代表律
　　师或者律师事务所签署。

风险代理费协议

66　（1）第 65 条适用于风险代理费协议。

（2）主管委员可以就风险代理费协议制定规则，包括但是不
　　　限于下列规则：

（a）限制律师或者律师事务所可以就其根据风险代理费

for services provided under contingent fee agreements;

(b) regulate the form and content of contingent fee agreements;

(c) set conditions to be met by lawyers and law firms making contingent fee agreements.

(3) Rules under subsection (2) apply only to contingent fee agreements made after the rules come into force and, if those rules are amended, the amendments apply only to contingent fee agreements made after the amendments come into force.

(4) A contingent fee agreement that exceeds the limits established by the rules is void unless approved by the court under subsection (6) .

(5) If a contingent fee agreement is void under subsection (4) , the lawyer may charge the fees that could have been charged had there been no contingent fee agreement, but only if the event that would have allowed payment under the void agreement occurs.

(6) A lawyer may apply to the court for approval of a fee higher than the rule permits, only

(a) before entering into a contingent fee agreement, and

(b) after serving the client with at least 5 days' written notice.

(7) The court may approve an application under subsection (6) if

(a) the lawyer and the client agree on the amount of the lawyer's proposed fee, and

(b) the court is satisfied that the proposed fee is reasonable.

(8) The following rules apply to an application under subsection

　　　　协议提供的服务收取的费用数额；

　　（b）规制风险代理费协议的形式和内容；

　　（c）设定律师和律师事务所签订风险代理费协议所要达
　　　　到的条件。

（3）（2）规定的规则仅适用于在规则生效后达成的风险代理
　　　费协议，如果这些规则被修正了，这些修正仅仅适用于
　　　在修正生效后达成的风险代理费协议。

（4）超过规则确立的限度的风险代理费协议无效，除非根据
　　　（6）得到法院批准。

（5）如果根据（4）风险代理费协议无效，律师可以收取在本
　　　没有风险代理费协议情况下可以收取的律师费，但是仅
　　　限于根据有效协议允许付款的情况。

（6）仅在下列情况下，律师可以申请法院批准高于规则所允
　　　许的律师费：

　　（a）达成风险代理费协议之前，以及

　　（b）至少在 5 日前向委托人送达书面通知。

（7）在下列情况下，法院可以批准（6）规定的申请：

　　（a）律师和委托人就律师准备收取的律师费达成协议，
　　　　并且

　　（b）法院确信准备收取的律师费是合理的。

（8）下列规则适用于（6）规定的保护事务律师—委托人特免

(6) to preserve solicitor client privilege:

(a) the hearing must be held in private;

(b) the style of proceeding must not disclose the identity of the lawyer or the client;

(c) if the lawyer or the client requests that the court records relating to the application be kept confidential,

(i) the records must be kept confidential, and

(ii) no person other than the lawyer or the client or a person authorized by either of them may search the records unless the court otherwise orders.

(9) Despite subsection (8) , reasons for judgment relating to an application under subsection (6) may be published if the names of the lawyer and client are not disclosed and any information that may identify the lawyer or the client is not disclosed.

Restrictions on contingent fee agreements

67 (1) This section does not apply to contingent fee agreements entered into before June 1, 1988.

(2) A contingent fee agreement must not provide that a lawyer is entitled to receive both a fee based on a proportion of the amount recovered and any portion of an amount awarded as costs in a proceeding or paid as costs in the settlement of a proceeding or an anticipated proceeding.

(3) A contingent fee agreement for services relating to a child guardianship or custody matter, or a matter respecting

权的申请：

（a）听证必须秘密举行；

（b）程序的风格不得披露律师或者委托人的身份；

（c）如果律师或者委托人请求对与该申请有关的法院记录加以保密，

　　（i）对记录必须保密，并且

　　（ii）律师或者委托人或者由二者授权的人员之外的任何人员都不得检索记录，除非法院另有命令。

（9）尽管（8），在律师和委托人的姓名不会披露，以及可以识别律师或者委托人的信息不被披露的情况下，可以公布作出与根据（6）提出的申请有关的判决的理由。

对风险代理费协议的限制

67　（1）本条并不适用于在 1988 年 6 月 1 日前达成的风险代理费协议。

　　（2）风险代理费协议不得规定律师有权既收取基于挽回的款项的比例收费，也收取程序中作为成本判赔的款额或者在程序或者预期程序的和解中作为成本支付的款项的任何部分。

　　（3）就与儿童监护或者抚养权事务，或者关于与子女相处时间、与子女的联系或者接触的事项有关的服务达成的风

parenting time of, contact with or access to a child, is void.

(4) A contingent fee agreement for services relating to a matrimonial dispute is void unless approved by the court.

(5) A lawyer may apply to the court for approval of a contingent fee agreement for services relating to a matrimonial dispute and section 66 (7) to (9) applies.

Examination of an agreement

68 (1) This section does not apply to agreements entered into before June 1, 1988.

(2) A person who has entered into an agreement with a lawyer or law firm may apply to the registrar to have the agreement examined.

(3) An application under subsection (2) may only be made within 3 months after

(a) the agreement was made, or

(b) the termination of the solicitor client relationship.

(4) Subject to subsection (3) , a person may make an application under subsection (2) even if the person has made payment under the agreement.

(5) On an application under subsection (2) , the registrar must confirm the agreement unless the registrar considers that the agreement is unfair or unreasonable under the circumstances existing at the time the agreement was entered into.

(6) If the registrar considers that the agreement is unfair or unreasonable under the circumstances existing at the time

险代理费协议无效。

（4）就与婚姻争端有关的服务达成的风险代理费协议无效，除非得到法院批准。

（5）律师可以申请法院批准就与婚姻争端有关的服务达成的风险代理费协议，就此适用 66（7）至（9）。

对协议的检查

68 （1）本条并不适用在 1988 年 6 月 1 日前达成的协议。

（2）与律师或者律师事务所达成协议的人员，可以向司法常务官申请对该协议进行检查。

（3）根据（2）提出的申请，仅可以在下列情况后 3 个月内提出：

（a）协议达成，或者

（b）事务律师—委托人关系终止。

（4）在遵守（3）的情况下，一个人可以根据（2）提出申请，即使该人根据协议已经付费。

（5）就根据（2）提出的申请，司法常务官必须确认该协议，除非司法常务官认为根据达成协议时存在的境况，该协议是不公平或者不合理的。

（6）如果司法常务官根据达成协议时存在的境况，认为该协议是不公平或者不合理的，司法常务官可以修改或者撤

the agreement was entered into, the registrar may modify or cancel the agreement.

(7) If an agreement is cancelled under subsection (6), a registrar

(a) may require the lawyer to prepare a bill for review, and

(b) must review the fees, charges and disbursements for the services provided as though there were no agreement.

(8) A party may appeal a decision of the registrar under subsection (5) or (6) to the court.

(9) The procedure under the Supreme Court Civil Rules for the assessment of costs, review of bills and examination of agreements applies to the examination of an agreement.

Lawyer's bill

69 (1) A lawyer must deliver a bill to the person charged.

(2) A bill may be delivered under subsection (1) by mailing the bill to the last known business or residential address of the person charged.

(3) The bill must be signed by or on behalf of the lawyer or accompanied by a letter, signed by or on behalf of the lawyer, that refers to the bill.

(4) A bill under subsection (1) is sufficient in form if it contains a reasonably descriptive statement of the services with a lump sum charge and a detailed statement of disbursements.

(5) A lawyer must not sue to collect money owed on a bill until

销该协议。

（7）如果根据（6）协议被撤销，司法常务官：

（a）可以要求律师准备账单用以审查，以及

（b）必须就所提供的服务审查律师费、手续费和支出，就像没有协议那样。

（8）当事人可以就司法常务官根据（5）或者（6）作出的决定，上诉于法院。

（9）《最高法院民事规则》规定的用于成本评定、账单审查和协议检查的程序，适用于对协议的检查。

律师的账单

69　（1）律师必须向被收费人提交账单。

（2）可以通过将账单邮寄给最后知道的被收费人的商业或者住宅地址，提交（1）规定的账单。

（3）账单必须由或者代表律师签字，或者附有由或者代表律师签字的提及该账单的信函。

（4）（1）规定的账单如果用收费总额和支出的详细说明合理描述了所提供的服务，在形式上就已经充分。

（5）律师不得起诉追讨账单欠款，直至账单提交给被收费人

30 days after the bill was delivered to the person charged.

(6) The court may permit a lawyer to sue to collect money owed on a bill before the end of the 30 days period if the court finds that

(a) the bill has been delivered as provided in subsection (1) , and

(b) there is probable cause to believe that the person charged is about to leave British Columbia other than temporarily.

Review of a lawyer's bill

70 (1) Subject to subsection (11) , the person charged or a person who has agreed to indemnify that person may obtain an appointment to have a bill reviewed before

(a) 12 months after the bill was delivered under section 69, or

(b) 3 months after the bill was paid,

whichever occurs first.

(2) The person who obtained an appointment under subsection (1) for a review of the bill must deliver a copy of the appointment to the lawyer at the address shown on the bill, at least 5 days before the date set for the review.

(3) Subject to subsection (11) , a lawyer may obtain an appointment to have a bill reviewed 30 days or more after the bill was delivered under section 69.

(4) The lawyer must serve a copy of the appointment on the person charged at least 5 days before the date set for the review.

30 日后。

（6）如果法院判定存在下列情况，法院可以允许律师在 30 日期间届满前起诉追讨账单欠款：

（a）已经按照（1）之规定提交了账单，以及

（b）有正当理由认为被收费人将要非临时性地离开不列颠哥伦比亚。

律师的账单的审查

70 （1）在遵守（11）的情况下，被收费人或者同意补偿该人的人员，可以在下列期日之前，获得预约来对账单进行审查：

（a）在根据第 69 条提交账单 12 个月后，或者
（b）在支付了账单 3 个月后，
以首先发生者为准。

（2）根据（1）就账单审查获得预约的人员，必须至少在确定的审查期日 5 日前，将预约复制件提交账单所列的律师的地址。

（3）在遵守（11）的情况下，在根据第 69 条提交账单后 30 日或者 30 日后，律师可以获得预约来就账单进行审查。

（4）律师必须至少在确定的审查期日 5 日前，将预约复制件送达被收费人。

(5) The following people may obtain an appointment on behalf of a lawyer to have a bill reviewed:

(a) the lawyer's agent;

(b) a deceased lawyer's personal representative;

(c) the lawyer's assignee;

(d) in the case of a partnership, one of the partners or a partner's agent;

(e) the custodian of the lawyer's practice appointed under section 50.

(6) If a lawyer has sued to collect on a bill, the court in which the action was commenced may order that the bill be referred to the registrar.

(7) The court may make an order under subsection (6) whether or not any party has applied for an order.

(8) On a referral under subsection (6) , the registrar may

(a) review the bill and issue a certificate, or

(b) make a report and recommendation to the court.

(9) When making an order under subsection (6) , the court may direct that the registrar take action under subsection (8) (a) or (b) .

(10) Section 73 applies to a certificate issued under subsection (8) (a) .

(11) In either of the following circumstances, the lawyer's bill must not be reviewed unless the court finds that special circumstances justify a review of the bill and orders that the bill be reviewed by the registrar:

(a) the lawyer has sued and obtained judgment for the

（5）下列人员可以代表律师获得预约来就账单进行审查：

　　（a）律师的代理人；

　　（b）已故律师的个人代表；

　　（c）律师的受让人；

　　（d）在合伙情况下，合伙人或者合伙人的代理人之一；

　　（e）根据第 50 条任命的律师执业活动的保管人。

（6）如果律师起诉就账单进行追讨，诉讼所在法院可以命令将该账单移送司法常务官。

（7）法院可以根据（6）作出命令，无论任何当事人是否申请了命令。

（8）就根据（6）进行的移送，司法常务官可以

　　（a）审查账单并开具证明，或者

　　（b）向法院作出报告和建议。

（9）在根据（6）作出命令时，法院可以指令司法常务官根据（8）（a）或者（b）采取行动。

（10）第 73 条适用于根据（8）（a）签发的证明。

（11）在任何下列情形下，不得审查律师账单，除非法院认定存在支持审查账单的特殊情形，并命令由司法常务官对账单进行审查：

　　（a）律师已经起诉，并就账单款额获得了判决；

amount of the bill;

(b) application for the review was not made within the time allowed in subsection (1).

(12) If a lawyer sues to collect money owed on a bill, the lawsuit must not proceed if an application for review is made before or after the lawsuit was commenced, until

(a) the registrar has issued a certificate, or

(b) the application for review is withdrawn.

(13) The procedure under the Supreme Court Civil Rules for the assessment of costs, review of bills and examination of agreements applies to the review of bills under this section.

(14) The registrar may refer any question arising under this Part to the court for directions or a determination.

Matters to be considered by the registrar on a review

71 (1) This section applies to a review or examination under section 68 (7), 70, 77 (3), 78 (2) or 79 (3).

(2) Subject to subsections (4) and (5), the registrar must allow fees, charges and disbursements for the following services:

(a) those reasonably necessary and proper to conduct the proceeding or business to which they relate;

(b) those authorized by the client or subsequently approved by the client, whether or not the services were reasonably necessary and proper to conduct the proceeding or business to which they relate.

（b）在（1）允许的时间内，没有提出审查申请。

（12）如果律师起诉追讨账单欠款，在诉讼开始之前或者之后提出了审查申请的情况下，诉讼不得继续进行，直至：

（a）司法常务官已经签发了证明，或者

（b）审查申请被撤回。

（13）《最高法院民事规则》就成本评定、账单审查和协议检查规定的程序，适用于根据本条进行的账单审查。

（14）司法常务官可以将根据本节产生的任何问题提交法院作出指示或者决定。

司法常务官在审查时考虑的事项

71　（1）本条适用于根据 68（7）、第 70 条、77（3）、78（2）或者 79（3）进行的审查或者询问。

（2）在遵守（4）和（5）的情况下，司法常务官必须就下列服务允许律师费、手续费和支出：

（a）在进行与之相关的程序或者业务时合理必需和适当的律师费、手续费和支出；

（b）委托人授权或者委托人随后批准的服务，无论该服务是否是进行与之相关的程序或者业务时合理必需和适当的。

(3) Subject to subsections (4) and (5) , the registrar may allow fees, charges and disbursements for the following services, even if unnecessary for the proper conduct of the proceeding or business to which they relate:

(a) those reasonably intended by the lawyer to advance the interests of the client at the time the services were provided;

(b) those requested by the client after being informed by the lawyer that they were unnecessary and not likely to advance the interests of the client.

(4) At a review of a lawyer's bill, the registrar must consider all of the circumstances, including

(a) the complexity, difficulty or novelty of the issues involved,

(b) the skill, specialized knowledge and responsibility required of the lawyer,

(c) the lawyer's character and standing in the profession,

(d) the amount involved,

(e) the time reasonably spent,

(f) if there has been an agreement that sets a fee rate that is based on an amount per unit of time spent by the lawyer, whether the rate was reasonable,

(g) the importance of the matter to the client whose bill is being reviewed, and

(h) the result obtained.

(5) The discretion of the registrar under subsection (4) is not limited by the terms of an agreement between the lawyer

（3）在遵守（4）和（5）的情况下，司法常务官可以下列服务允许律师费、手续费和支出，即使对于适当进行与之相关的程序或者业务而言并非必需：

（a）在提供这些服务时，律师旨在合理地促进委托人的利益；

（b）在律师告知它们是不必要的且不可能促进委托人的利益后，委托人要求这些服务。

（4）在审查律师账单时，司法常务官必须考虑所有情况，包括：

（a）所涉及的问题的复杂性、困难性或者新奇性，

（b）所需要的律师的技能、专业知识和责任，

（c）律师在职业中的品性和地位，

（d）所涉及的款额，

（e）合理花费的时间，

（f）是否存在这样的协议，即确定费率基于律师花费的时间的单位数额，无论该费率是否合理，

（g）事务对于其账单被审查的委托人的重要性，以及

（h）所获得的结果。

（5）（4）规定的司法常务官的裁量权，不受律师与律师的委托人之间的协议条款的限制。

and the lawyer's client.

Costs of a review of a lawyer's bill

72 (1) Costs of a review of a lawyer's bill must be paid by the following:

(a) the lawyer whose bill is reviewed, if 1/6 or more of the total amount of the bill is subtracted from it;

(b) the person charged, if less than 1/6 of the total amount of the bill is subtracted from it;

(c) a person who applies for a review of a bill and then withdraws the application for a review.

(2) Despite subsection (1) , the registrar has the discretion, in special circumstances, to order the payment of costs other than as provided in that subsection.

Remedies that may be ordered by the registrar

73 (1) On the application of a party to a review under this Part, the registrar may order that a party

(a) be permitted to pay money in instalments on the terms the registrar considers appropriate, or

(b) not be permitted to collect money on the certificate for a period the registrar specifies.

(2) On a review under this Part, the registrar may

(a) give a certificate for the amount the registrar has allowed the lawyer for fees, charges and disbursements, and

对律师的账单进行审查的成本

72 （1）对律师的账单进行审查的成本必须由下列人员支付：

   （a）账单受审查的律师，如果其账单总额的 1/6 或者更多
        被从中削减；

   （b）被收费人，如果不足账单总额的 1/6 被从中削减；

   （c）申请审查账单但是之后撤回审查申请的人员。

   （2）尽管有（1）之规定，司法常务官在特殊情形下，有自由
        裁量权来命令支付该款规定之外的成本。

司法常务官可以命令的救济措施

73 （1）就当事人根据本节提出的审查申请，司法常务官可以命令：

   （a）允许当事人按照司法常务官认为适当的条件分期付
        款，或者

   （b）不允许当事人在司法常务官具体规定的期间内追讨
        证明上所载的款项。

   （2）在根据本节进行审查时，司法常务官可以：

   （a）就司法常务官已经允许律师收取的律师费、手续费
        和支出的数额出具证明，以及

(b) summarily determine the amount of the costs of the review and add it to or subtract it from the amount shown on the certificate.

(3) If a registrar gives a certificate under subsection (2) , the registrar must add to the amount certified an amount of interest calculated

(a) on the amount the registrar has allowed the lawyer for fees, charges and disbursements, exclusive of the costs of the review,

(b) from the date the lawyer delivered the bill to the date on which the certificate is given, and

(c) at the rate agreed to by the parties at the time the lawyer was retained or, if there was no agreement, at the same rate the registrar would allow under the Court Order Interest Act on an order obtained by default.

(4) If a registrar gives a certificate under subsection (2) that requires that the lawyer refund money to another person, the registrar must add to the amount to be refunded an amount of interest calculated

(a) on the amount the lawyer is required to refund to the other person,

(b) from the date the money to be refunded was paid to the lawyer to the date on which the certificate is given, and

(c) at the same rate the registrar would allow under the Court Order Interest Act on an order obtained by default.

（b）速决确定进行审查的成本的数额，可以对证明载明
　　　的数额进行加减。

（3）如果司法常务官根据（2）作出了证明，司法常务官必须
　　　就所证明的款额判加计算的利息：

（a）该利息以司法常务官允许律师收取的律师费、手续
　　　费和支出为依据，但是不包括成本审查的成本，

（b）从律师提交账单之日到作出证明之日计算，以及

（c）按照聘请律师时双方商定的利率计算，或者在不存
　　　在该协议的情况下，按照司法常务官就默认获得的
　　　命令根据《法院判令利息法》可以允许的同样的利
　　　率计算。

（4）如果司法常务官根据（2）开具证明，要求律师向他人退
　　　款，司法常务官必须就所退回的款额判加计算的利息：

（a）该计算基于律师需要向他人退回的款额计算，

（b）从所退款项支付给律师之日到开具证明之日，以及

（c）按照司法常务官就默认获得的命令根据《法院判令
　　　利息法》可以允许的同样的利率计算。

Refund of fee overpayment

74 A lawyer must, on demand,

(a) refund fees, charges and disbursements received or retained in excess of the amount allowed under this Part or the rules, and

(b) pay any interest added under section 73 (4) .

Appeal

75 (1) A party to a review may appeal to the court, within

(a) 14 days from the date the certificate of the registrar was entered,

(b) the period the court may permit, or

(c) the period the registrar specifies at the time of signing the certificate.

(2) On the appeal, the court may make any order it considers appropriate.

(3) If the terms of an order of the court require it, the registrar must amend the certificate.

Registrar's certificate

76 (1) If it appears to the registrar that there is money due from the lawyer to the person charged, the registrar may make an interim certificate as to the amount payable by the lawyer.

(2) If an interim certificate is entered under subsection

退还多付费用

74　经请求，律师必须，

　　（a）退还收到的或者持有的超过根据本节或者规则所允许数额的律师费、手续费和支出，以及

　　（b）支付根据 73（4）计算的任何利息。

上诉

75　（1）审查的当事人可以在下列期间内向法院提起上诉：

　　（a）司法常务官出具证明之日起 14 日内，

　　（b）法院可能允许的期间，或者

　　（c）司法常务官在出具证明时具体规定的期间。

　　（2）在上诉中，法院可以作出其认为适当的任何命令。

　　（3）如果法院作出的命令的条款作出要求，司法常务官必须修正其证明。

司法常务官的证明

76　（1）如果在司法常务官看来，律师对被收费人有欠款，司法常务官可以就律师应付的款额开具临时证明。

　　（2）如果根据（1）开具了临时证明，法院可以命令所证明的

(1) , the court may order the money certified to be paid immediately

(a) to the person charged, or

(b) into court.

(3) After a review under sections 70 and 71, the certificate of the registrar may be filed in a registry of the court and, on the expiry of the time specified or permitted under section 75, the certificate is deemed to be a judgment of the court.

Order to deliver bill or property

77 (1) The court may order, on terms it considers appropriate, delivery of a bill to the person charged, if

(a) a bill has not been delivered, and

(b) the bill, if it had been delivered, could have been the subject of an application for a review under section 70.

(2) A person charged may apply to the court for an order that the client's lawyer or former lawyer deliver to the court, to the client or to the client's agent

(a) an accounting,

(b) property, or

(c) a list of any property of the client in the lawyer's control.

(3) When an order under subsection (2) is made, the court may

(a) order the review of the lawyer's bill and require the person charged to pay or secure the lawyer's claim before delivery is made, and

款额立即支付给:

（a）被收费人，或者

（b）法院。

（3）在根据第 70 条和第 71 条进行审查后，司法常务官的证明可以提交法院登记处，在具体规定的时间或者第 75 条允许的时间届满后，该证明被视为是法院的判决。

命令提交账单或者财产

77 （1）在下列情况下，法院可以命令，按照其认为适当的条件，将账单提交被收费人:

（a）账单还没有被提交，以及

（b）账单，如果被提交，将根据第 70 条被申请审查。

（2）被收费人可以向法院申请命令，要求委托人的律师或者前律师向法院、委托人或者委托人的代理人提交:

（a）账目，

（b）财产，或者

（c）律师控制下的委托人的任何财产的清单。

（3）在根据（2）作出命令时，法院可以

（a）命令审查律师的账单，并要求被收费人在提交之前，就律师的主张付款或者提供担保，以及

(b) relieve the lawyer of any undertakings given or any other responsibilities in relation to the property.

Change of lawyer

78 (1) If a client changes lawyers or begins acting on his or her own behalf, the client or the new lawyer may apply to the court for an order directing that the client's former lawyer deliver the client's records to another lawyer nominated by the client or to the client, as the case may be.

(2) If the court makes an order under subsection (1) , the court may

(a) make the direction conditional on the client

(i) paying all amounts due to the client's former lawyer from the client, or

(ii) giving security for the payment of the lawyer's claim in an amount and manner satisfactory to the court, and

(b) order a review by the registrar.

Lawyer's right to costs out of property recovered

79 (1) A lawyer who is retained to prosecute or defend a proceeding in a court or before a tribunal has a charge against any property that is recovered or preserved as a result of the proceeding for the proper fees, charges and disbursements of or in relation to the proceeding, including counsel fees.

（b）使律师免于作出任何承诺或者与财产有关的任何其他责任。

更换律师

78 （1）如果委托人更换律师，或者开始自行代理，委托人或者新律师可以向法院申请命令，指令委托人的前律师将委托人的记录移送委托人提名的另一个律师或者委托人，视情况而定。

（2）如果法院根据（1）作出了命令，法院可以：

（a）就作出的指令以委托人下列行为为条件：

（i）委托人向其前律师支付全部欠款，或者

（ii）就律师主张的支付，以令法院满意的方式提供担保，以及

（b）命令由司法常务官进行审查。

律师从追回的财产中取得成本的权利

79 （1）被聘请在法院程序或者裁判庭程序中起诉或者辩护的律师，就追回的任何财产或者作为程序的结果留存的任何财产，可以收回程序的或者与之相关的适当律师费、手续费和支出，包括法律顾问费。

(2) Subsection (1) applies whether or not the lawyer acted as counsel.

(3) The court that heard the proceeding or in which the proceeding is pending may order the review and payment of the fees, charges and disbursements out of the property as that court considers appropriate.

(4) Sections 70 to 73 apply to a review under subsection (3) of this section.

(5) If the proceeding referred to in subsection (1) was before a tribunal, the lawyer may apply to the court for an order under subsection (3) .

(6) All acts done and conveyances made to defeat, or that operate or tend to defeat, the charge are void against the charge, unless made to a bona fide purchaser for value without notice.

(7) A proceeding for the purpose of realizing or enforcing a charge arising under this section may not be taken until after application has been made to the appropriate court for directions.

（2）无论律师是否担任法律顾问，（1）都适用。

（3）听审程序的法院或者程序所系属的法院，可以命令审查并从财产中支付其认为适当的律师费、手续费和支出。

（4）第 70 条至第 73 条适用于根据本条（3）进行的审查。

（5）如果（1）所称程序是在裁判庭之前进行的，律师可以根据（3）向法院申请命令。

（6）旨在不支付索费或者其运作会致使索费无着的所有行为和财产转移活动，就该索费而言无效，除非是未经通知的善意取得人。

（7）为实现或者执行根据本条提出的索费的程序不得提起，直至向适当法院申请指令后。

Part 9 Incorporation

Definitions

80   In this Part:

"limited liability partnership" means a partnership registered as a limited liability partnership under Part 6 of the Partnership Act;

"permit" means a permit issued under section 82 and includes a permit and a renewal of a permit issued to a law corporation or personal law corporation under the Legal Profession Act, R.S.B.C. 1996, c. 255.

Authorized and prohibited activities of law corporations

81   (1) A law corporation is authorized to carry on the business of providing legal services to the public through one or more persons each of whom is

(a) a practising lawyer, or

(b) subject to this Act and the rules, a person referred to in section 15 (1) (c) , (e) or (f) or (2) who is an employee of the law corporation.

(2) A partnership consisting of law corporations or of one or more lawyers and one or more law corporations is authorized to

第 9 节　公司

定义

80　在本节中：

"有限责任合伙" 是指根据《合伙法》第 6 节登记为有限责任合伙的合伙；

"许可证" 是指根据第 82 条签发的许可证，包括根据《法律职业法（R.S.B.C. 1996, c. 255）》签发给法律公司或者个人法律公司的许可证和续展的许可证。

法律公司的受权和被禁止活动

81　（1）法律公司受权通过一个或者多个下列人员开展向公众提供法律服务的业务活动：

（a）执业律师，或者

（b）在遵守本法和规则的情况下，15（1）（c）、（e）或者（f）或者（2）所称的作为法律公司的雇员的人员。

（2）由法律公司或者一个或者多个律师与一个或者多个法律公司组成的合伙，有权通过（1）规定的一个或者多个人

carry on the business of providing legal services to the public through one or more persons described in subsection (1) .

(3) A corporation that has the words "law corporation" as part of its name must not carry on any business unless it holds a valid permit.

(4) A law corporation must not carry on any activities, other than the provision of legal services or services directly associated with the provision of legal services.

(5) Subsection (4) does not prohibit a law corporation from investing its funds in real estate, personal property, mortgages, stocks, bonds, insurance or any other type of investment.

(6) A voting trust agreement, proxy or any other type of agreement vesting in a person who is not a practising lawyer or a law corporation the authority to exercise the voting rights attached to shares in a law corporation is prohibited.

Law corporation permit

82　(1) The executive director must issue a permit to a corporation that is a company, as defined in the Business Corporations Act, and that is in good standing under that Act or that is an extra provincial company as defined in that Act, if the executive director is satisfied that

(a) the corporation has complied with the rules made under this Part,

(b) the name of the corporation includes the words "law

员开展向公众提供法律服务的业务活动。

（3）其名称含有"法律公司"字样的公司，不得开展任何业务活动，除非它持有有效许可证。

（4）除了提供法律服务或者提供与法律服务直接相关的服务，法律公司不得开展任何活动。

（5）（4）并不禁止法律公司将其资金投资于动产、不动产、抵押贷款、股票、债券、保险，或者进行任何其他类型的投资。

（6）禁止投票信托协议、委托书或者任何其他类型的协议向不是执业律师或者法律公司的人员授予法律公司股份投票权。

法律公司许可证

82 （1）如果执行主任确信下列情况，执行主任必须向《商业公司法》界定的根据该法资格完好的公司或者该法界定的省外公司签发许可证：

（a）该公司遵守了根据本节制定的规则，

（b）公司的名称包括"法律公司"字样，

corporation",

(c) each voting share is legally and beneficially owned by a practising lawyer or by a law corporation,

(d) each non-voting share is legally and beneficially owned by

(i) a practising lawyer,

(ii) a law corporation that is a voting shareholder,

(iii) a person who is a relative of or resides with a practising lawyer who is a shareholder or who is a shareholder in a law corporation that is a shareholder,

(iv) a corporation, all the shares of which are beneficially owned by one or more of the individuals referred to in subparagraph (i) or (iii), or

(v) a trust, all the beneficiaries of which are individuals referred to in subparagraph (i) or (iii),

(e) all of the directors and the president of the corporation are practising lawyers, and

(f) all of the persons who will be practising law on behalf of the corporation are persons described in section 81 (1).

(2) The executive director may refuse to issue a permit under subsection (1) if

(a) the law corporation has previously had its permit revoked, or

(b) a shareholder of the law corporation was a shareholder of a law corporation or personal law corporation that

（c）每个有表决权的股份都在法律上和实益上为执业律师或者法律公司所有，

（d）每个无表决权的股份都在法律上和实益上由下列人员或者公司所有：

（ⅰ）执业律师，

（ⅱ）作为有表决权的股东的法律公司，

（ⅲ）与是股东或者是作为股东的法律公司的股东的执业律师的亲属或者与之同居的人员，

（ⅳ）公司，其所有股份在实益上由（ⅰ）或者（ⅲ）所称的一个或者多个自然人所有，或者

（ⅴ）信托，其所有受益人都是（ⅰ）或者（ⅲ）所称的自然人，

（e）公司的所有董事和董事长都是执业律师，以及

（f）所有将代表公司从事法律执业活动的人员，都是 81（1）规定的人员。

（2）在下列情况下，执行主任可以拒绝颁发（1）规定的许可证：

（a）法律公司以前曾经被吊销许可证，或者

（b）法律公司的股东是以前曾经被吊销许可证的法律公司或者个人法律公司的股东。

previously had its permit revoked.

(3) The executive director must inform the Registrar of Companies of the revocation of any permit under this Part or the rules.

(4) Unless the benchers otherwise direct and subject to rules made under this Part, if a law corporation fails to pay the renewal fee set by the benchers by the date it is due, its permit ceases to be valid and the corporation must

(a) immediately surrender its permit to the executive director, and

(b) cease providing legal services to the public.

Law corporation rules

83 (1) The benchers may make rules as follows:

(a) establishing procedures for the issue and renewal of permits;

(b) establishing procedures for revocation of permits, including

(i) the adaptation of rules respecting practice and procedure in hearings before a panel, and

(ii) rules to authorize a panel to consider action against a law corporation as part of a hearing on a citation issued against a respondent who is or was a shareholder, director, officer or employee of a law corporation;

(c) authorizing the executive director to attach conditions

（3）执行主任必须就根据本节或者规则吊销任何许可证，通知公司登记官。

（4）除非主管委员另有指示，且遵守根据本节制定的规则，如果法律公司未按照主管委员确定的期日支付续展规费，其许可证不再有效，公司必须：

（a）立即将其许可证上交执行主任，并且

（b）停止向公众提供法律服务。

法律公司规则

83 （1）主管委员可以制定下列规则：

（a）建立颁发和续展许可证的程序；

（b）建立吊销许可证的程序，包括：

（i）就专责小组举行的听证的操作和程序制定规则，以及

（ii）通过规则授权专责小组作为针对是或者曾经是法律公司的股东、董事、职员或者雇员的应诉人签发的传唤证的听证的一部分，考虑针对法律公司的行动；

（c）授权执行主任就根据本节颁发或者续展的许可证设

or limitations to permits issued or renewed under this Part;

(d) respecting names and the approval of names including the types of names by which the following may be known, be incorporated or practise law:

   (i) a law corporation;

   (ii) a partnership consisting of one or more law corporations and one or more lawyers;

   (iii) a partnership consisting of law corporations;

   (iv) a law corporation that has shareholders that consist of one or more law corporations or one or more practising lawyers, or both;

(e) setting fees for

   (i) obtaining a permit, and

   (ii) renewing a permit;

(f) respecting the disposition of shares of a shareholder of a law corporation who ceases to be a practising lawyer;

(g) setting an amount of insurance that the holder of the permit must carry or must provide to each of its employees or contractors for the purpose of providing indemnity against professional liability claims;

(h) any other rules the benchers consider necessary or advisable for the purposes of this Part.

(2) The amount set by a rule made under subsection (1) (g) is in addition to any amount that must be carried by a lawyer under a rule made under section 30 (1.1), and the amount that may be set under this subsection may be

　　　定条件或者限制；

　（d）下列实体具有为人所知、注册成立或者开展法律执
　　　　业活动的名称、名称的核准，包括名称的类型：

　　　（ⅰ）法律公司；
　　　（ⅱ）由一个或者多个法律公司和一个或者多个律师
　　　　　　组成的合伙；
　　　（ⅲ）由法律公司组成的合伙；
　　　（ⅳ）其股东由一个或者多个法律公司或者一个或者
　　　　　　多个执业律师或者二者构成的法律公司；

　（e）就下列事项确定规费：
　　　（ⅰ）获得许可证，以及
　　　（ⅱ）续展许可证；
　（f）法律公司的不再是执业律师的股东的股份的处置；

　（g）确定许可证持有者必须持有或者必须为其每个雇员
　　　　或者订约人为就职业责任索赔进行赔偿目的所提供
　　　　的保险额；

　（h）主管委员认为为本节之目的有必要或者可取的任何
　　　　其他规则。
（2）根据（1）（g）制定的规则所确定的数额，是除了律师根
　　　据依 30（1.1）制定的规则必须持有的任何数额之外的数
　　　额，根据本款可以确定的数额，可以就不同的许可证持
　　　有者而有所不同，由主管委员酌定。

different for different permit holders, at the discretion of the benchers.

(3) An act of a corporation, including a transfer of property to or by the corporation, is not invalid because it contravenes this Part or the rules made under this Act.

(4) This Act and the rules apply, insofar as is possible, to law corporations in the same way that they do to individual lawyers.

Limited liability partnerships

83.1   The benchers may make rules

(a) authorizing lawyers and law corporations to carry on the practice of law through limited liability partnerships, and

(b) establishing prerequisites, conditions, limitations and requirements for lawyers and law corporations to carry on the practice of law through limited liability partnerships.

Responsibility of lawyers

84   (1) The liability of a lawyer, carrying on the practice of law, for his or her own professional negligence is not affected by the fact that the lawyer is carrying on that practice

(a) as an employee, shareholder, officer, director or contractor of a law corporation or on its behalf, or

(b) through a limited liability partnership.

(2) The application of the provisions of this Act and the rules to a lawyer is not affected by the lawyer's relationship to

（3）公司的行为，包括向或者由公司转移财产，并不因为其
　　违反了本节或者根据本法制定的规则而无效。

（4）在可能的情况下，本法和规则像适用于自然人律师那样，
　　适用于法律公司。

有限责任合伙

83.1　主管委员可以制定规则：

（a）授权律师和法律公司通过有限责任合伙开展法律执业
　　活动，以及

（b）就律师和法律公司通过有限责任合伙开展法律执业活
　　动确定先决条件、条件、限制和要求。

律师的责任

84　（1）律师就其开展法律执业活动所要自行承担的职业过失责
　　　任，不受这样的事实的影响：

（a）律师在作为法律公司的雇员、股东、职员、董事或
　　者订约人开展该执业活动，或者

（b）律师在通过有限责任合伙开展该执业活动。

（2）本法和规则的规定对律师的适用，不受律师下列关系的
　　影响：

(a) a law corporation as an employee, shareholder, officer, director or contractor, or

(b) a limited liability partnership as a partner, employee or contractor.

(3) Nothing in this Part affects, modifies or limits any law applicable to the fiduciary, confidential or ethical relationships between a lawyer and a person receiving the professional services of the lawyer.

(4) The relationship between a law corporation carrying on business as authorized under this Part and the rules, and a person receiving legal services provided by the corporation is subject to all applicable law relating to the fiduciary, confidential and ethical relationships that exist between a lawyer and a client.

(5) All rights and obligations respecting professional communications made to or information received by a lawyer, or in respect of advice given by a lawyer, apply to a law corporation and its employees, shareholders, officers, directors and contractors.

(6) An undertaking given by or on behalf of a law corporation that would constitute a solicitor's undertaking if given by a lawyer is deemed to be a solicitor's undertaking given by the lawyer who gives, signs or authorizes it.

（a）作为雇员、股东、职员、董事或者订约人与法律公司的关系，或者

（b）作为合伙人、雇员或者订约人与有限责任合伙的关系。

（3）本节并不影响、修改或者限制适用于律师与接受律师的职业服务的人员之间的受托、秘密或者道德关系的任何法律。

（4）根据本节和规则开展受权业务的法律公司与接受该公司提供的法律服务的人员之间的关系，要遵守与律师和委托人之间存在的受托、保密和道德关系有关的所有现行法律。

（5）与向律师作出的职业交流或者律师收到的信息、律师所提供的建议有关的所有权利和义务，适用于法律公司及其雇员、股东、职员、董事和订约人。

（6）由或者代表法律公司作出的如果是律师作出的将构成事务律师的承诺的承诺，视为作出、签署或者授权它的律师作出的事务律师的承诺。

Part 10   General

Enforcement

85 (1) A person commits an offence if the person

    (a) contravenes section 15, or

    (b) uses or discloses information contrary to section 88 (3) or (4) .

(2) If an offence under this Act is committed by a corporation, each director, manager, secretary or other officer of that corporation who has assented to the commission of the offence is a party to that offence.

(3) An information alleging an offence against this Act may be laid in the name of the society on oath or by affirmation of the executive director or of a person authorized by the benchers.

(4) Section 5 of the Offence Act does not apply to this Act or to the rules.

(5) The society may apply to the Supreme Court for an injunction restraining a person from contravening this Act or the rules.

(6) The court may grant an injunction sought under subsection

第 10 节 一般规定

执行

85 （1）一个人如果存在下列情形，则构成犯罪：

（a）违反第 15 条，或者

（b）违反 88（3）或者（4）使用或者披露信息。

（2）如果本法规定的犯罪是公司实施的，每个同意实施该犯罪的董事、经理、秘书或者该公司的其他职员，都是该犯罪的当事人。

（3）诉称违反本法的犯罪的起诉书，可以以律师协会名义，在执行主任或者主管委员授权的人员宣誓或者郑重陈述后提出。

（4）《犯罪法》第 5 条并不适用于本法或者规则。

（5）律师协会可以向最高法院申请禁令，制止某人违反本法或者规则。

（6）法院如果确信有理由认为已经或者将会发生违反本法或

(5) if satisfied that there is reason to believe that there has been or will be a contravention of this Act or the rules.

(7) The court may grant an interim injunction until the outcome of an action commenced under subsection (5) .

(8) On the application of the society or a person interested in the proceeding, the court in which a proceeding is brought may find a person in breach of section 15 (5) to be in contempt and may punish that person accordingly.

Protection against actions

86   (1) No action for damages lies against a person, for anything done or not done in good faith while acting or purporting to act on behalf of the society or the foundation under this Act.

(2) The society or the foundation, as the case may be, must indemnify a person referred to in subsection (1) for any costs or expenses incurred by the person in any legal proceedings taken for anything done or not done in good faith while acting or purporting to act on behalf of the society or the foundation under this Act.

Certain matters privileged

87   (1) In this section:

"proceeding" does not include a proceeding under Part 2, 3, 4 or 5;

"report" includes any document, minute, note, correspondence or memorandum created or received by a person, committee, panel, review

者规则的行为，可以发出根据（5）申请的禁令。

（7）法院可以发出临时禁令，直至根据（5）开始的行动有了结果。

（8）经律师协会或者程序中的利害关系人的申请，该程序所在法院可以认定违反 15（5）的人构成藐视法庭，并可以对该人进行处罚。

针对诉讼的保护

86　（1）根据本法代表律师协会或者基金会采取行动或者宣称代表其行动时所做的任何事情的人员，无论是否出于善意，都不得就造成的损害对该人起诉。

（2）律师协会或者基金会（视情况而定），必须就（1）所称根据本法代表律师协会或者基金会采取行动或者宣称代表其行动时的人员因就对其所做的任何事情（无论是否出于善意）提起的法律程序所引起的任何成本或者耗费，对该人员进行补偿。

受特免权保护的某些事项

87　（1）在本条中：

"**程序**"并不包括根据第 2 节、第 3 节、第 4 节或者第 5 节进行的程序；

"**报告**"包括一个人、委员会、专责小组、审查委员会或者律师协会代理人在调查、审计、审查或者听证过程中形成的或者收到的任何文

board or agent of the society in the course of an investigation, audit, inquiry or hearing, but does not include an original document that belongs to a complainant or respondent or to a person other than an employee or agent of the society.

(2) If a person has made a complaint to the society respecting a lawyer, neither the society nor the complainant can be required to disclose or produce the complaint and the complaint is not admissible in any proceeding, except with the written consent of the complainant.

(3) If a lawyer responds to the society in respect of a complaint or investigation, neither the lawyer nor the society can be required to disclose or produce the response or a copy or summary of it and the response or a copy or summary of it is not admissible in any proceeding, except with the written consent of the lawyer, even though the executive director may have delivered a copy or a summary of the response to the complainant.

(4) A report made under the authority of this Act or a record concerning an investigation, an audit, an inquiry, a hearing or a review must not be required to be produced and is not admissible in any proceeding except with the written consent of the executive director.

(5) Except with the written consent of the executive director, the society, an employee or agent or former employee or agent of the society, or a member or former member of a committee, panel or review board established under this Act

(a) must not be compelled to disclose information that

件、会议记录、笔记、通信或者备忘录，但是并不包括属于投诉人或者应诉人或者律师协会的雇员或者代理人之外的人员的原件。

（2）如果一个人就律师向律师协会提出了投诉，不得要求律师协会或者投诉人披露或者出示投诉，该投诉在任何程序中不可采，得到投诉人书面同意者除外。

（3）如果律师就投诉或者调查对律师协会作出回应，不得要求该律师或者律师协会披露或者出示该回应或者该回应的复制件或者摘要，该回应或者该回应的复制件或者摘要在任何程序中不可采，得到律师书面同意者除外，即使执行主任可以向投诉人提交该回应的复制件或者摘要。

（4）根据本法授权制作的报告或者关于调查、审计、审查、听证或者审查的记录，不得被要求出示，且在任何程序中不可采，执行主任作出书面同意者除外。

（5）除非执行主任作出书面同意，律师协会、律师协会的雇员或者代理人、前雇员或者代理人、根据本法建立的委员会、专责小组或者审查委员会的成员或者前成员：

（a）不得被迫披露该人在调查、审计、审查、听证或者

the person has acquired during the course of an investigation, an audit, an inquiry, a hearing or a review or in the exercise of other powers or the performance of other duties under this Act, and

(b) is not competent to testify in a proceeding if testifying in that proceeding would result in the disclosure of information referred to in paragraph (a) .

Non–disclosure of privileged and confidential information

88 (1) [Repealed 2012-16-46 (a) .]

(1.1) A person who is required under this Act or the rules to provide information, Files or records that are confidential or subject to a solicitor client privilege must do so, despite the confidentiality or privilege.

(1.2) Information, files or records that are provided in accordance with subsection (1.3) are admissible in a proceeding under Part 2, 3, 4 or 5 of this Act, despite the confidentiality or privilege.

(1.3) A lawyer who or a law firm that, in accordance with this Act and the rules, provides the society with any information, files or records that are confidential or subject to a solicitor client privilege is deemed conclusively not to have breached any duty or obligation that would otherwise have been owed to the society or the client not to disclose the information, files or records.

(2) Despite section 14 of the Freedom of Information and

复查或者在行使本法规定的其他权力或者履行本法
规定的其他职责的过程中获得的信息，以及

（b）如果在程序中作证将导致披露（a）所称的信息，则
无在该程序中作证的资格。

不得披露受特免权保护的信息和秘密信息

88 （1）［废止 2012-16-46（a）.］

（1.1）根据本法或者规则被要求提供秘密的或者受事务律师—
委托人特免权保护的信息、卷宗或者记录的人员，必须
这么做，尽管存在该秘密性或者特免权。

（1.2）遵照（1.3）提供的信息、卷宗或者记录在根据本法第 2
节、第 3 节、第 4 节或者第 5 节提起的程序中可采，尽
管存在秘密性或者特免权。

（1.3）遵照本法和规则向律师协会提供了秘密的或者受事务律
师—委托人特免权保护的信息、卷宗或者记录的律师或
者律师事务所，结论性地被视为并没有违反可能本对律
师协会或者委托人承担的不披露信息、卷宗或者记录的
职责或者义务。

（2）尽管有《信息自由和隐私保护法》第 14 条之规定，一个

Protection of Privacy Act, a person who, in the course of exercising powers or carrying out duties under this Act, acquires information, files or records that are confidential or are subject to solicitor client privilege has the same obligation respecting the disclosure of that information as the person from whom the information, files or records were obtained.

(3) A person who, during the course of an investigation, audit, inquiry or hearing under this Act, acquires information or records that are confidential or subject to solicitor client privilege must not disclose that information or those records to any person except for a purpose contemplated by this Act or the rules.

(4) A person who, during the course of an appeal under section 48 or an application under the Judicial Review Procedure Act respecting a matter under this Act, acquires information or records that are confidential or are subject to solicitor client privilege must not

(a) use the information other than for the purpose for which it was obtained, or

(b) disclose the information to any person.

(5) The Court of Appeal, on an appeal under section 48, and the Supreme Court, on an application under the Judicial Review Procedure Act respecting a matter under this Act, may exclude members of the public from the hearing of the appeal or application if the court considers the exclusion is necessary to prevent the disclosure of information, files or

人在根据本法行使权力或者履行职责过程中获得了秘密
的或者受到事务律师—委托人特免权保护的信息、卷宗
或者记录，像提供该信息、卷宗或者记录的人一样，就
披露这些信息有同样的义务。

（3）在根据本法进行的调查、审计、审查或者听证过程中，
获得了秘密的或者受事务律师—委托人特免权保护的信
息或者记录的人员，不得向任何人披露该信息或者记录，
本法或者规则规定的目的除外。

（4）在就本法规定事项根据第 48 条提出的上诉或者根据《司
法审查程序法》提出的申请期间，获得了秘密的或者受
事务律师—委托人特免权保护的信息或者记录的人员，
不得

（a）为获得这些信息之外的目的使用这些信息，或者

（b）向他人披露该信息。

（5）如果法院认为退庭为防止披露秘密的或者受事务律师—
委托人特免权保护的信息、卷宗或者记录所必需，上诉
法院在根据第 48 条提起的上诉听证中，以及最高法院在
就本法规定事项根据《司法审查程序法》提出的申请听
证中，可以要求公众退庭。

records that are confidential or subject to solicitor client privilege.

(6) In giving reasons for judgment on an appeal or application referred to in subsection (5) , the Court of Appeal or the Supreme Court must take all reasonable precautions to avoid including in those reasons any information before the court on the appeal or application that is confidential or subject to solicitor client privilege.

(7) Despite section 14 of the Freedom of Information and Protection of Privacy Act, the benchers may make rules for the purpose of ensuring the non-disclosure of any confidential information or information that, but for this Act, would be subject to solicitor client privilege, and the rules may be made applicable to any person who, in the course of any proceeding under this Act, would acquire the confidential or privileged information.

(8) Section 47 (4) of the Freedom of Information and Protection of Privacy Act does not apply to information that, but for this Act and the production of the information to the commissioner under that Act, would be subject to solicitor client privilege.

Repealed

89 [Repealed 2012-16-47.]

（6）在就（5）所称的上述或者申请的判决给出理由时，上诉
　　法院或者最高法院必须采取所有合理预防措施，以避免
　　在这些理由中包括在向法院提出的上诉或者申请中涉及
　　的秘密或者受事务律师—委托人特免权保护的任何信息。

（7）尽管有《信息自由与隐私保护法》第 24 条之规定，主管
　　委员可以制定规则，以确保除了为本法目的外，不披露
　　任何秘密信息或者受事务律师—委托人特免权保护的信
　　息，规则可以在本法规定的任何程序中适用于获得了秘
　　密或者受特免权保护的信息的任何人员。

（8）《信息自由和隐私保护法》47（4）并不适用于受事务律
　　师—委托人特免权保护的信息，为本法目的和根据该法
　　向专员提供信息者除外。

废止

89　［废止 2012-16-47.］

Service

90 The benchers may make rules respecting service of documents under this Act.

Law society insurance

91 (1) The benchers may purchase and maintain insurance protecting the society, the benchers, officers and employees of the society and former benchers, officers and employees against liability arising out of the operations or activities of the society and providing for indemnity with respect to any claims arising out of acts done or not done by those individuals in good faith while acting or purporting to act on behalf of the society.

(2) The benchers may enter into, on behalf of members, contracts of life, accident, income replacement and any other type of insurance that they consider will benefit the members.

Legal archives

92 (1) The benchers may make rules permitting a lawyer or law firm to deposit records in the possession of the lawyer or law firm in an archives, library or records management office in Canada.

(2) Rules made under this section may provide for

送达

90　主管委员可以就根据本法送达文件制定规则。

律师协会保险

91　（1）主管委员可以购买和维持保险，以保护律师协会、主管
委员、律师协会的职员和雇员、前主管委员、职员和雇
员免于承担律师协会的运营或者活动引发的责任，就这
些人在代表或者宣称代表律师协会行为时的作为或者不
作为所引发的任何索赔提供赔偿。

（2）主管委员可以代表会员就人寿、事故、收入替代和其他
类型的保险达成他们认为属于会员福利的合同。

法律档案

92　（1）主管委员可以制定规则，允许律师或者律师事务所将律
师或者律师事务所持有的记录存放在加拿大的档案馆、
图书馆或者记录管理办公室。

（2）根据本条制定的规则可以就下列事项作出规定：

(a) the time after which the records may be deposited,

(b) the restrictions or limitations on public access that the lawyer or law firm may attach on depositing them, and

(c) circumstances under which the lawyer or law firm cannot be liable for disclosure of confidential or privileged information arising out of the deposit.

（a）经历多久后可以存放这些记录，

（b）律师或者律师事务所就公众近用这些记录可以在存
放时设定的限制，以及

（c）律师或者律师事务所并不对因存放而导致秘密的或
者受特免权保护的信息披露承担责任的情形。

Part 11   Transitional and Consequential Provisions

Repealed

93 [Repealed 2012-16-49.]

Spent

94–108 [Repeal, consequential amendments and amendments to this Act. Spent. 1998-9-94 to 108.]

Commencement

109   This Act comes into force by regulation of the Lieutenant Governor in Council.

第 11 节　过渡性和相应规定

废止

93　［废止 2012-16-49.］

失效

94—108　［本法的废止、相应修正和对本法的修正。失效。1998-9-
94 to 108.］

施行

109　本法经省督的条例生效。

Legal Profession Act

[SBC 1998] CHAPTER 9

Changes Not in Force

Section	Change	Citation	Into force
1	am	2012–16–1 (b)	by reg
26	am	2012–16–15 (a)	by reg
34	am	2012–16–23	by reg
35	am	2009–22–57	by reg (2009–22–99 as am by 2014–9–29)
36	am	2012–16–24 (a)	by reg
37	am	2012–16–25	by reg
38	am	2012–16–27 (a) , (b) , (d) , (i) , (j)	by reg
41	am	2012–16–30	by reg
42	am	2012–16–31 (a) , (d)	by reg
47	am	2012–16–36 (b)	by reg
50	am	2009–22–58	by reg (2009–22–99 as am by 2014–9–29)
61	am	2012–16–38 (b)	by reg
62	am	2012–16-39	by reg
63	am	2012–16–40	by reg
87	am	2012–16–45 (c)	by reg
87	am	2012–16–45 (d) (part)	by reg

立法变动表

[SBC 1998] 第 9 章

尚未生效的变动

条	变动	出处	生效方式
1	修正	2012–16–1（b）	经条例
26	修正	2012–16–15（a）	经条例
34	修正	2012–16–23	经条例
35	修正	2009–22–57	经条例（2009–22–99，已经被 2014–9–29 修正）
36	修正	2012–16–24（a）	经条例
37	修正	2012–16–25	经条例
38	修正	2012–16–27（a），（b），（d），（i），（j）	经条例
41	修正	2012–16–30	经条例
42	修正	2012–16–31（a），（d）	经条例
47	修正	2012–16–36（b）	经条例
50	修正	2009–22–58	经条例（2009–22–99，已经被 2014–9–29 修正）
61	修正	2012–16–38（b）	经条例
62	修正	2012–16–39	经条例
63	修正	2012–16–40	经条例
87	修正 修正	2012–16–45（c） 2012–16–45（d）（部分）	经条例 经条例

Changes in Force

Section	Change	Citation	Effective date
1	am am	2009–13–235 2016–5–41, Sch 3	31Mar 2014（BC Reg 148/2013） 10 Mar 2016（RA）
19, 20, 26.01	am	2016–5–41, Sch 3	10 Mar 2016（RA）
30	am am	2016–5–43, Sch 5 2016–5–44, Sch 6	10 Mar 2016（RA） 10 Mar 2016（RA）
38 , 39, 42	am	2016–5–41, Sch 3	10 Mar 2016（RA）
61	am	2015–1–96	24 Jun 2015（BC Reg 114/2015）
73	am	2016–5–44, Sch 6	10 Mar 2016（RA）

生效的变动

条	变动	出处	生效期日
1	修正 修正	2009–13–235 2016–5–41，附录 3	2014 年 3 月 31 日（不列颠哥伦比亚条例 148/2013） 2016 年 3 月 10 日（御准）
19, 20, 26.01	修正	2016–5–41，附录 3	2016 年 3 月 10 日（御准）
30	修正 修正	2016–5–43，附录 5 2016–5–44，附录 6	2016 年 3 月 10 日（御准） 2016 年 3 月 10 日（御准）
38,39, 42	修正	2016–5–41，附录 3	2016 年 3 月 10 日（御准）
61	修正	2015–1–96	2015 年 6 月 24 日（不列颠哥伦比亚条例 114/2015）
73	修正	2016–5–44，附录 6	2016 年 3 月 10 日（御准）

重要译名对照表

Admission	准入
Advocate	诉辩者
Articled student	见习生
Assessment	摊款 评定
Bencher	主管委员
Benchers	主管委员会
Call	认许
Charge	索费 收费 手续费
Conduct unbecoming a lawyer	与律师身份不相称的行为
Credential	资质
Custodian	保管人
Deed of settlement	财产处分契据
Delegate	委派 委派代表
Discipline	惩戒
Fee	律师费 规费
Foundation	基金会
Good standing	资格完好
Governor	理事
Governing body	治理组织
Instrument	文书
Insurance adjuster	保险精算人

Law clerk	法律助手
Medical examination	医学检查
Member	会员
Notary public	公证人
Panel	专责小组
Person charged	被收费人
Practice	业务 业务活动
Practising certificate	执业证书
Prepaid legal services plan	预付法律服务计划
Rescission	废除
Respondent	应诉人
Sheriff	治安官
Suspension	停止执业
Trust deed	信托契据
Reinstatement	恢复执业
Letter of request	证据要求书
Law corporation	法律公司
Permit	许可证
Privilege	特权 特免权

图书在版编目（CIP）数据

加拿大不列颠哥伦比亚省1998年法律职业法 / 王进喜译. —北京：中国法制出版社，2017.5

ISBN 978-7-5093-8565-4

Ⅰ. ①加… Ⅱ. ①王… Ⅲ. ①律师法—加拿大 Ⅳ. ① D971.165

中国版本图书馆 CIP 数据核字（2017）第 104640 号

责任编辑　袁笋冰　欧　丹　　　　　　　　　　封面设计　李　宁

加拿大不列颠哥伦比亚省 1998 年法律职业法
JIANADABULIEDIAN GELUNBIYASHENG 1998NIAN FALÜZHIYEFA
译者 / 王进喜
经销 / 新华书店
印刷 / 北京京华虎彩印刷有限公司
开本 / 710 毫米 × 1000 毫米　16 开　　　　　印张 / 15.5　字数 / 208 千
版次 / 2017 年 6 月第 1 版　　　　　　　　　　2017 年 6 月第 1 次印刷

中国法制出版社出版

书号 ISBN 978-7-5093-8565-4　　　　　　　　　　　　　定价：48.00 元

北京西单横二条 2 号　　　　　　　　　　　　　　值班电话：66026508
邮政编码：100031　　　　　　　　　　　　　　　　传真：66031119
网址：http://www.zgfzs.com　　　　　　　　　　编辑部电话：66066621
市场营销部电话：66033393　　　　　　　　　　邮购部电话：66033288

（如有印装质量问题，请与本社编务印务管理部联系调换。电话：010-66032926）